Gibbon

Past Masters

AQUINAS Anthony Kenny
ARISTOTLE Jonathan Barnes
BACH Denis Arnold
FRANCIS BACON Anthony Quinton
BAYLE Elisabeth Labrousse
BERKELEY J. O. Urmson
THE BUDDHA Michael Carrithers
BURKE C. B. Macpherson
CARLYLE A. L. Le Quesne
CHAUCER George Kane
CLAUSEWITZ Michael Howard
COBBETT Raymond Williams
COLERIDGE Richard Holmes
CONFUCIUS Raymond Dawson
DANTE George Holmes
DARWIN Jonathan Howard
DIDEROT Peter France
GEORGE ELIOT Rosemary Ashton
ENGELS Terrell Carver
GALILEO Stillman Drake
GIBBON J. W. Burrow
GOETHE T. J. Reed
HEGEL Peter Singer

HOMER Jasper Griffin
HUME A. J. Ayer
JESUS Humphrey Carpenter
KANT Roger Scruton
LAMARCK L. J. Jordanova
LEIBNIZ G. MacDonald Ross
LOCKE John Dunn
MACHIAVELLI Quentin Skinner
MARX Peter Singer
MENDEL Vitezslav Orel
MONTAIGNE Peter Burke
THOMAS MORE Anthony Kenny
WILLIAM MORRIS Peter Stansky
MUHAMMAD Michael Cook
NEWMAN Owen Chadwick
PASCAL Alban Krailsheimer
PETRARCH Nicholas Mann
PLATO R. M. Hare
PROUST Derwent May
RUSKIN George P. Landow
ADAM SMITH D. D. Raphael
TOLSTOY Henry Gifford
WYCLIF Anthony Kenny

Forthcoming

AUGUSTINE Henry Chadwick
BERGSON Leszek Kolakowski
JOSEPH BUTLER R. G. Frey
CERVANTES P. E. Russell
COPERNICUS Owen Gingerich
DESCARTES Tom Sorell
DISRAELI John Vincent
ERASMUS John McConica
GODWIN Alan Ryan
HERZEN Aileen Kelly
JEFFERSON Jack P. Greene
JOHNSON Pat Rogers
KIERKEGAARD Patrick Gardiner
LEONARDO E. H. Gombrich

LINNAEUS W. T. Stearn
MILL William Thomas
MONTESQUIEU Judith Shklar
NEWTON P. M. Rattansi
ROUSSEAU Robert Wokler
RUSSELL John G. Slater
ST PAUL G. B. Caird
SHAKESPEARE Germaine Greer
SOCRATES Bernard Williams
SPINOZA Roger Scruton
VICO Peter Burke
VIRGIL Jasper Griffin
and others

J. W. Burrow

Gibbon

Oxford   New York
OXFORD UNIVERSITY PRESS
1985

Oxford University Press, Walton Street, Oxford OX2 6DP

London New York Toronto
Delhi Bombay Calcutta Madras Karachi
Kuala Lumpur Singapore Hong Kong Tokyo
Nairobi Dar es Salaam Cape Town
Melbourne Auckland

and associated companies in
Beirut Berlin Ibadan Mexico City Nicosia

Oxford is a trade mark of Oxford University Press

First published 1985 as an Oxford University Press paperback
and simultaneously in a hardback edition

British Library Cataloguing in Publication Data

Burrow, J. W.
Gibbon. — (Past masters)
1. Gibbon, Edward   2. Historians—
England—Biography
I. Title   II. Series
937'.0072024   DG206.G5
ISBN 0-19-287553-1
ISBN 0-19-287552-3 Pbk

Set by Grove Graphics
Printed in Great Britain by
Cox & Wyman Ltd, Reading

To Patrick Mullin
for forty years' friendship

Contents

Acknowledgements

My first debt in connection with this book is to Larry Siedentop for suggesting that I should write it. Most of the actual writing was done in the History of Ideas Unit of the Australian National University, which did me the honour to elect me into a Visiting Fellowship. I am particularly grateful to the Director and members of the Unit, and to other members of the Research School of Social Sciences of the ANU, for the warmth of their welcome and the stimulus and geniality of their company, which did much to mitigate the rigours of composition. For reading the manuscript and making helpful criticisms and suggestions I am grateful to Charles Burrow, Stefan Collini, Ruth Morse, Quentin Skinner, John Thompson, and Donald Winch. They must not, of course, be blamed for any errors which may have slipped through. I am also grateful to Kay Smith, who typed the manuscript.

In addition I should like to thank the General Editor of the series, Keith Thomas, for his criticisms and suggestions, and Henry Hardy and his colleagues at the Oxford University Press for their help.

Abbreviations

The editions of Gibbon's works quoted in the text are cited as follows:

The History of the Decline and Fall of the Roman Empire ed. J. B. Bury, 6th ed. (London, 1912), 7 vols. Cited by volume number and page

S   *An Essay on the Study of Literature.* Translated from the French. Facsimile of 1st ed. Printed New York, 1970

M   *Memoirs of my Life and Writings*, ed. Georges A. Bonnard (London, 1966)

J   *Gibbon's Journal to January 28th, 1763*, ed. D. M. Low (London, 1929)

L   *The Letters of Edward Gibbon*, ed. J. E. Norton, 3 vols. (London, 1956)

W   *The Miscellaneous Works of Edward Gibbon Esq.*, ed. Lord Sheffield, 2 vols, (London, 1796). Additional vol. 1815

A   *The Autobiography of Edward Gibbon*, published by Oxford University Press in the World's Classics series; 1907 edition

1 Conception

In the middle of the eighteenth century the ruins of ancient Rome became, in the works of Italian topographical artists such as Pannini and Piranesi, a favourite source of picturesque imagery. Through their engravings, rather than in the remains of the Forum and the Capitol today, we can begin to recreate the impression then made by ancient Rome on the English tourist: the ruins standing in the silence and neglect of their desolation, offering, as it seemed, moralizing contrasts between the endless vitality of mere nature and the decay of human works—broken columns lying overgrown with tangles of briars; vegetation spurting through cracked marble; oxen trampling the political heart of an empire which had extended from the Firth of Forth to the Nile cataracts and from the borders of Persia to the Atlantic coast of North Africa. To the classically educated visitor, meditation on the mutability of greatness and the fall of empires was almost an obligation. Virgil, in his *Aeneid*, had given his hero Aeneas, a refugee from Troy and the founder of Rome, a vision of the future city. Now, with the turn of fortune's wheel, the site of the Forum and the Capitol seemed to be returning again to the rural simplicity in which Aeneas had first seen it, and where he had been granted his vision of its future glories.

Edward Gibbon, making his only visit to Italy in 1764, at the age of twenty-seven, had no difficulty in summoning up an appropriate awe, and joined to it a sense of exalted wonder at his own arrival at the sacred spot. As he wrote many years later in his posthumously published *Memoir*,

My temper is not very susceptible of enthusiasm, and the enthusiasm which I do not feel I have ever scorned to affect. But at the distance of twenty five years I can neither forget nor express the strong emotions which agitated my mind as I first approached and entered the *eternal city*. After a sleepless night I trod with a lofty step the ruins of the Forum; each memorable spot where Romulus *stood*, or Tully spoke, or Caesar fell was at once present to my eye; and several days of intoxication were lost or enjoyed before I could descend to a cool and minute investigation. (M 134)

It was not just hindsight: he wrote at the time to his father with an equivalent enthusiasm, if in less studied phrases: 'I am really almost in a dream' (L 184).

It was, as every reader of Gibbon knows, in this critical confrontation that he found his life's work, his fame, and even, in the latter part of his life, his sense of his own identity: 'the historian of the Roman empire'. Again it is, as so often, impossible to resist quoting his own words: 'It was at Rome on the fifteenth of October 1764, as I sat musing amidst the ruins of the Capitol while the barefooted friars were singing Vespers in the temple of Jupiter, that the idea of writing the decline and fall of the City first started to my mind' (M 134 n.4).

Like many famous historical episodes, it cannot, it seems, have been quite like that. The temple of Jupiter was, slightly less impressively, the temple of Juno—the Church of S. Maria in Ara Coeli. Gibbon's journal of the period, to which one version of his *Memoir* explicitly refers as the source of his recollection, contains no record of the event, and according to the testimony of his companion, they visited no ruins that day; it rained and they went to look at pictures. But if Gibbon, as seems likely, compressed into a single episode a number of different scenes and impressions, it hardly matters. Through *The History of the Decline and Fall of the Roman Empire* and his famous account of its conception, Gibbon has attached his own name, ineffaceably, to what he called in the conclusion of the *History* itself, 'the greatest, perhaps, and most awful scene in the history of mankind' (7.325). The Capitol has become the spot where Tully spoke and Caesar fell and Gibbon mused. Indeed, it has become more the last than the first; many now who have scarcely heard of Tully, even under his more familiar name of Cicero, know of Gibbon's *Decline and Fall*, perhaps the most famous work of history ever written, and of its kind the greatest. It is our good fortune that it was written in English, and such an English as no one else has written. It might easily have been in French, for Gibbon was bilingual. To read it is no light undertaking. It covers twelve centuries, three continents, and, in the standard modern edition, seven volumes. But the rewards are immense. Thomas Carlyle, the historian of the French Revolution and a man who, apart from his vocation, shared with Gibbon scarcely a single quality or sympathy, said of him, 'Gibbon is a kind of bridge that connects the antique with the modern ages. And how gorgeously does it swing across the gloomy and multitudinous chasm of those barbarous centuries . . . The perusal of his work forms an epoch in the history of one's mind.'

2 Life

Gibbon is the author not of one masterpiece but of two, a vast canvas and an exquisite miniature. The second, the *Memoir* of his life, was written in the leisured contentment of the brief period between the completion of the history and his death. The studied felicity of Gibbon's phrasing has made it surely the most quoted autobiography in the English language, and it was, in fact, very carefully composed. Gibbon wrote six different drafts, and seems to have been equivocal about whether he wished to publish it in his lifetime. It was edited, rather drastically, and published after his death by his friend Lord Sheffield. Gibbon's autobiography, as it is most commonly known, is not an exercise in intimate self-revelation like Rousseau's *Confessions* (the two men, predictably, disliked each other). It is a study of the creation of 'the historian of the Roman empire', as Gibbon had come proudly and justly to call himself, whose earlier episodes could be seen as unconscious preparation, or as checks and snares which might have aborted the great work, all circumvented by judgement or good fortune. Gibbon, in retrospect, obviously enjoyed contemplating the chances against the successful completion of his life's work, and he never forgot that he had been fortunate as well as dedicated.

> My lot might have been that of a slave, a savage, or a peasant; nor can I reflect without pleasure on the bounty of Nature, which cast my birth in a free and civilized country, in an age of science and philosophy, in a family of honourable rank and decently endowed with the gifts of fortune. (M 24 n.1)

But the strong element of conscious art does not mean that we have to regard Gibbon's autobiography as a distortion; only that, like any biography or autobiography, it gives us a selected version which we can sometimes check against his letters and journals. Nevertheless, much more than most men's, Gibbon's life had actually become a deliberate composition, devoted, in its latter part, with little or no deviation, to the achievement of a single great task. And if Gibbon, in the afterglow of achievement, smoothed a little his youthful anxieties and frustrations, he did not conceal them entirely. For the reader who simply wants the salient facts about Gibbon's life, the *Memoir* is an adequate guide as well as a source of continuing delight.

Early life

The genealogy Gibbon provides for himself in the *Memoir* is largely conjectural. The important figure, the founder of the family fortunes and therefore our benefactor as well as his, is his paternal grandfather, an army clothing contractor during the French wars at the beginning of the eighteenth century, who lost his fortune in the disaster of the South Sea Bubble, and then made another. It was this that enabled Gibbon's father to assume the rank of a country gentleman, to enter Parliament, and to marry the daughter of a London merchant, Judith Porten. Edward Gibbon, born in 1737 and named after his father, was their eldest and only surviving child. He was sickly and not expected to live, and believed he owed his life to the care and nursing of his aunt Catherine Porten, who became a second mother to him. It was to her too, 'the true mother of my mind as well as of my health', that he ascribed his 'early and invincible love of reading, which I would not exchange for the treasures of India' (M 36). He particularly remembered his introduction to Pope's translation of Homer and to the *Arabian Nights*; he was later to become an insatiable reader of books of travel as well as of history, and always retained a keen interest in the Orient. Because of his frequent illnesses his schooling was scrappy. At a private school 'By the common methods of discipline, at the expense of many tears and some blood, I purchased the knowledge of the Latin syntax.' A brief period at Westminster School followed, but his classical languages never achieved the polish of 'a well-flogged critic' (M 38); his Latin remained inexact and his Greek, at this point, rudimentary. In 1752, miscellaneously well-read but intellectually undisciplined, he went up to Magdalen College, Oxford, 'with a stock of erudition that might have puzzled a Doctor, and a degree of ignorance of which a school boy would have been ashamed' (M 43).

Gibbon's strictures on Oxford and on the dons among whom he spent fourteen idle and unprofitable months have become classic:

> From the toil of reading or thinking, or writing they had absolved their conscience . . . Their conversation stagnated in a round of College business, Tory politics, personal stories and private scandal: their dull and deep potations excused the intemperance of Youth; and their constitutional toasts were not expressive of the most lively loyalty for the house of Hanover. (M 52–3)

His tutor, Dr Winchester, whose name was suppressed in Sheffield's edition, has been immortalized in an antithesis: 'Dr—— well remembered that he had a salary to receive, and only forgot that he had a duty to perform' (M 56–7).

Catholicism and Lausanne

Intellectually eager but unguided, with the desire he had

conceived to study Arabic discouraged, Gibbon took what seemed at the time, and indeed in a sense proved, a fateful step: 'From my childhood I had been fond of religious disputation . . . The blind activity of idleness urged me to advance without armour into the dangerous mazes of controversy; and at the age of sixteen, I bewildered myself in the errors of the Church of Rome' (M 58). Gibbon's conversion to Catholicism was characteristically bookish; he knew no Catholic; he read himself into the Catholic Church. The first step was a reaction against a controversial book of the period, Conyers Middleton's *A Free Inquiry into the Miraculous Powers which are supposed to have existed in the Christian Church* (1748). Middleton, adding the boldness of the eighteenth-century Enlightenment to traditional Protestant suspicion of Catholic superstitions and deceptions, had criticized the miracles of the early Church. The young Gibbon was not ready for such freedom, but in rejecting it he found himself drawn into belief not merely in the miracles but in the virtue and truth of the Catholic Church by and for whom the miracles had been performed. The miracles of the early Church always required a nice distinction by Protestants, who believed in the miracles of the Gospels and the Acts of the Apostles, but distrusted or rejected the 'superstitious' legends of the Catholic saints. Where was the line to be drawn? Gibbon found that Middleton's attack provoked him into wholesale endorsement. He went on to the Catholic apologetics of the great seventeenth-century French bishop, Bossuet; he was converted, 'and I surely fell by a noble hand' (M 59), though he also told Lord Sheffield that the writings of the Elizabethan Jesuit, Robert Parsons, had been crucial.

In June 1753, in London, Gibbon was received into the Catholic Church by a priest from the Sardinian embassy.

He at once announced the fact with some bravado to his father, and the matter became public knowledge. Oxford, still a closed Anglican religious body, was barred to him, and all his career prospects were blighted.

His father acted promptly and decisively, and at the end of a fortnight Gibbon had left England, dispatched to live in Lausanne in the house of a Calvinist minister, M. Pavilliard. His circumstances were unenviable.

> I had now exchanged my elegant apartment in Magdalen College for a narrow, gloomy street, the most unfrequented of an unhandsome town, for an old inconvenient house, and for a small chamber ill-contrived and ill-furnished, which on the approach of winter instead of a companionable fire must be warmed by the dull, invisible heat of a stove. From a man I was again degraded to the dependence of a school-boy. (M 70)

Moreover, he spoke no French. It was not precisely martyrdom, but for a youth of sixteen accustomed to comfort, it was bleak enough.

Pavilliard, however, turned out to be a sensible and humane man and Gibbon came to respect him; he was in every respect an improvement on the tutors at Magdalen. In these unpromising surroundings Gibbon's mind developed and his education became more securely grounded. He stayed in Lausanne for five years, growing fluent in Latin and more at home in French than English. Pavilliard handled the task of his religious reconversion adroitly, and by the end of 1754 Gibbon was again, 'with full conviction', a Protestant. He read widely, by now with more discipline and application, in logic and in the philosophy of Locke, in the historians and jurists of the seventeenth and eighteenth centuries, Grotius, Bayle, and Montesquieu, and in the Latin classics, above all in Cicero.

In the latter 'I tasted the beauties of language, I breathed the spirit of freedom, and I imbibed from his precepts and examples the public and private sense of a man' (M 75 n. 7). Locke's *Treatise of Civil Government* (*sic*) 'instructed me in the knowledge of Whig principles' (M 78); the political creed of the Gibbon family was Tory, tinged with Jacobitism, for which Gibbon had suffered at the hands of his schoolfellows at the time of the 1745 Jacobite rising. Gibbon also met Voltaire, then established in Switzerland, though he offended the great man by circulating an unpublished poem by Voltaire without permission; relations between the two were never more than polite, and in later years Gibbon became a severe critic of Voltaire's superficial scholarship. Gibbon also began Greek again, picking his way painfully, with Pavilliard's help, through the *Iliad*, 'and I had the pleasure of beholding, though darkly and through a glass, the true image of Homer, whom I had long since admired in an English dress, and also working at the Greek historians, Herodotus and Xenophon' (M 77).

These years in Lausanne were of incalculable importance to Gibbon. As he recognized, they were the 'fortunate banishment' which saved him from 'port and prejudice among the monks of Oxford' (M 209). They gave him a further five years of education, this time under the supervision of a conscientious tutor and free from the distractions of a country, town, or university life in England. They made all French literature available to him and made him a citizen of Europe. They laid the foundations for Gibbon the scholar, though it was not yet clear in precisely which direction his bent would take him. The most serious crisis of these years, his love affair with Suzanne Curchod, who later married the Swiss banker and minister of Louis XVI, Necker, and became the mother of

Mme de Staël, is now chiefly remembered for Gibbon's epigrammatic summing-up after his father had forbidden marriage: 'I sighed as a lover; I obeyed as a son' (M 85 n.7). The affair was perhaps more painful than this terseness implies, but readers of the *Decline and Fall* have cause to be grateful to Gibbon's father. Mlle Curchod had no money, and as her husband Gibbon would have had to lead a different kind of life. All the same, it is tantalizing to speculate what we might have had instead of Germaine de Staël.

England: the militia

In 1758 Gibbon's father allowed him to return to England. The next five years, until his father gave him the money to make his fateful Grand Tour through France and Italy in 1763, were a period of at least superficial idleness and of somewhat bizarre activity. Lausanne had made him a scholar; London made him in due course a man of the world; his father's home at Buriton (also spelt Beriton) in Hampshire wholly failed to make him a country gentleman or sportsman. In the country his hours of study were constantly interrupted by the demands of eighteenth-century genteel sociability, 'and in the midst of an interesting work I was often called down to receive the visit of some idle neighbours' (M 96). In London he began the book purchases which laid the foundations of what was eventually to be a library of some six thousand volumes: 'I cannot forget the joy with which I exchanged a bank-note of twenty pounds for the twenty volumes of the Memoirs of the Academy of Inscriptions; nor would it have been easy, by any other expenditure of the same sum, to have procured so large and lasting a fund of rational amusement' (M 97).

The most incongruous episode of Gibbon's life, however, was about to begin, an odd by-product of the war with France. The event is best told in Gibbon's own words:

A national militia has been the cry of every patriot since the Revolution; and this measure, both in the parliament and in the field, was supported by the country gentlemen or Tories, who insensibly transferred their loyalty to the house of Hanover . . . In the act of offering our names and receiving our commissions, as major and captain in the Hampshire regiment, we had not supposed that we should be dragged away, my father from his farm, myself from my books, and condemned during two years and a half, to a wandering life of military servitude . . . When the King's order for our embodying came down, it was too late to retreat, and too soon to repent. (A 104) (This passage is omitted from Bonnard's edition but included in Sheffield's.)

From 1760 to 1762 Gibbon and his battalion marched from camps and quarters through the southern counties of England. Even during this wandering life Gibbon's journal is witness to an impressive amount of reading in the classics and history, as well as, more predictably, to the formidable drinking of an eighteenth-century militia officers' mess. He even found time to resume the serious study of Greek. With his usual retrospective cheerfulness, he found some blessings even in this heavy disguise: 'The discipline and evolutions of a modern battalion gave me a clearer notion of the phalanx and the legion; and the captain of the Hampshire grenadiers (the reader may smile) has not been useless to the historian of the Roman empire' (M 117). More importantly, and probably truthfully, he said that his militia service, after his foreign education, made an Englishman of him again. It was in the years of his renewed

11

English residence, too, (though he still often wrote in French) that he first steeped himself in the literature of Augustan England, and particularly Swift and Addison: 'The favourite companions of my leisure were our English writers since the Revolution; they breathe the spirit of reason and liberty; and they most seasonably contributed to restore the purity of my own language, which had been corrupted by the long use of a foreign idiom' (M 98). When Gibbon came to write the *Decline and Fall*, it was in his own distinctive version of the language, and guided by the principles, of a late-Augustan Englishman, not as a French *philosophe* only fortuitously writing in English.

Grand Tour: 'the historian of the Roman empire'

The end of the war brought not only freedom from the militia but also the possibility of foreign travel, and Gibbon seized it eagerly. Within a matter of weeks, in early 1763, he was in Paris. The account of his literary projects and publications will be better left to the next chapter, but it was relevant at this point that his first publication, in 1761, an essay in French on the study of literature, had brought him a modest reputation as a man of letters. The salons of Paris were opened to him by this and by various introductions, and he was able to meet the most eminent of the *philosophes*, the intellectual leaders of the French Enlightenment: Diderot and D'Alembert, Helvétius and D'Holbach, as well as scholars he admired and whose work he was later to use, such as the Abbé de la Bléterie, who had written an impressive study of the Emperor Julian the Apostate, and another scholar, de Guignes, to whose work on the Huns Gibbon would one day be greatly indebted. He also looked at manuscript collections in the public libraries, though he never learned to read them. His attitude to the *philosophes* was rather reserved; he saw in them an intolerant atheistic zeal which his own cooler temperament found uncongenial.

In May he was once again in Lausanne, this time willingly. Almost a year later, after preparing himself exhaustively for Rome, by taking copious notes on the classic descriptions of ancient Italy, on modern studies of Italian antiquities, and on the topography of the ancient capital, he crossed the Alps and made his way by leisurely stages to his goal. We have already considered his account of that first, momentous confrontation. In June 1765 he returned to London, and to the most frustrating five years of his life. Now approaching thirty, he had begun to chafe at his father's authority and to pine for independence. Outwardly these years were marked only by one or two publications of ephemeral interest. He had no profession, and his father's extravagance threatened all his prospects. Though his relations with his father had become cordial, he hardly denies that the latter's death in 1770 was a form of deliverance.

In the years which followed, though he had begun the composition of the *Decline and Fall*, whose first volume appeared in 1776, he still thought in terms of a career. His fortune was not large and life in London was expensive. From these London years come some of our best descriptions of Gibbon by his contemporaries: the chubby, tiny figure—he was less than 5 feet tall—somewhat overdressed, his manner studied to the point of affectation, his mouth a small round hole in his round face, from which issued the elaborately flowing periods of his conversation. In 1774 he was elected to The Club, the famous dining club founded by Dr Johnson, which also included Oliver Goldsmith, David Garrick, Sir Joshua Reynolds, Adam Smith, Edmund Burke, and James Boswell. Gibbon and

Johnson did not get on; Johnson's roughness and Gibbon's urbanity were ill-matched; the latter found Garrick and Reynolds more congenial, and had his revenge on Johnson in caustic footnotes in the *Decline and Fall*. Boswell called Gibbon 'an ugly, affected, disgusting fellow'.

Through the influence of his kinsman Lord Eliot, a cousin by marriage, Gibbon was able to enter Parliament as Member for Liskeard in 1774. It was a golden age of English parliamentary eloquence, and Gibbon listened, in the debates over the revolt of the American colonies, to the oratory of Burke, Sheridan, and Fox. His own hopes were soon dashed by the discovery that he had neither the talent nor the courage of an orator: 'prudence condemned me to acquiesce in the humble station of a mute' (M 156). But his silent support for Lord North's government in the division lobbies, and a pamphlet in French vindicating the English conduct towards France brought him the reward of a parliamentary career that he had hoped for, a place. The historian of the Roman empire became one of the Lords Commissioners of Trade and Plantations at a salary of over seven hundred pounds a year. Then a turn of the wheel of parliamentary fortune determined the pattern of the last part of Gibbon's life. The movement for economical reform mounted by the opposition Whigs extinguished Gibbon's place, and the extra income was lost. He decided to abandon his parliamentary career and in 1783, as a measure of economy, he migrated to Lausanne, to the home of his Swiss friend Deyverdun, which eventually became his own. Here, in a summer-house in the garden overlooking Lake Leman, the last part of the *Decline and Fall* was written.

Gibbon never regretted his decision. His last years in Lausanne were soured only by the death of Deyverdun and the outbreak of the French Revolution. Gibbon, who had once written a pamphlet against the oligarchy of the Canton of Bern, in which Lausanne lay, abhorred the revolutionaries. They were, as he wrote significantly in a letter, 'The new Barbarians who labour to confound the order and happiness of society' (L 3.321). In the *Memoir* they are pictured in a phrase recalling another kind of actor in the *Decline and Fall*, 'the fanatic missionaries of sedition' (M 185). Gibbon recoiled from 'the Gallic phrenzy' and greeted Burke's *Reflections on the Revolution in France* with enthusiasm.

European uncertainties and the fatal illness of the wife of his friend Lord Sheffield brought Gibbon back to England for a visit in 1793. While in London he was operated on for a long-standing complaint, a hydrocele, or testicle grossly swollen by dropsy. After a short but grisly illness, on 19 January 1794, at Sheffield Place in Sussex, he died, and he is buried in the Sheffield family vault in the parish church at the nearby village of Fletching.

3 Vocation

The Essay on the Study of Literature

'I know by experience that from my early youth,' Gibbon wrote in his *Memoir*, 'I aspired to the character of an historian' (M 119). His first published work, which appeared in French in 1761 and in an English translation immediately afterwards, is entitled *An Essay on the Study of Literature*, but in it 'literature' is construed widely to include not only the classics but history and scholarship generally. It sets out to defend this 'literature' against the neglect or contempt that Gibbon felt characterized the attitude of some of his contemporaries, particularly in France. In making such a defence, he was defining his own future vocation, and he was not altogether wrong in thinking that a defence was necessary. It is at first sight paradoxical that Gibbon, who, at least until the outbreak of the French Revolution, was on such good terms with his own 'enlightened age', as he sometimes called it, and who epitomized in himself so much of its culture and so many of its beliefs, should have written his earliest work as a protest against what he saw as one of its most powerful intellectual currents: scorn for the past and an exaltation of wit, elegance and reason over scholarship.

Not that the *Essay* is in any way a work of excessively partisan, youthful zeal. On the contrary, it was a characteristically Gibbonian plea for moderation, and a protest against what he saw as the excesses of the 'philosophic' enthusiasm of the eighteenth-century Enlightenment with its belief in reason, progress and science. Gibbon was himself a man of the Enlightenment, and 'philosophy' and 'philosophic' in this eighteenth-century sense are used by him invariably with approval, but he disapproved of a facile dismissal of the value of the Greek and Latin classics, and the achievements of Renaissance and seventeenth-century scholars. Gibbon's approving use of 'philosophy' is significant, but so is the scornful footnote reference in the *Decline and Fall* to a modern author 'who quotes nobody, according to the last fashion of the French writers' (7.91 n.19)—a remark of more than eighteenth-century application.

Gibbon was later to be a severe critic of his youthful essay. It has indeed the failings he diagnosed: 'The most serious defect of my Essay is a kind of obscurity and abruptness which always fatigues, and may often elude the attention of the reader . . . the sense of the word *littérature* is loosely and variously applied: a number of remarks and examples, historical, critical, philosophical, are heaped on each other without method or connection' (M 103). Gibbon wrote it in French, because that was the language in which he then thought, and to procure a wider readership. It did in fact have considerably more success in France than in England, where it was largely ignored. The English translation (not by Gibbon) was faulty and clumsy, but Gibbon came to feel that even in the original his style, under the influence of Montesquieu, whom he greatly admired, was excessively terse and epigrammatic. But the substance of the *Essay* Gibbon did not disclaim, and had no reason to, at any period of his life. It took up the stance towards history and scholarship, and also towards 'philosophy' as his century understood it, as the critical use of reason and the search for the underlying causes or 'principles' of things, that he was to hold throughout his career. The synthesis for which he argued in the essay was the one he came triumphantly to embody. The programme

17

it very briefly and scrappily set out for the 'philosophic historian' to follow was a juvenile sketch of the mature Gibbon. When later he applied the philosophic, rational impulse of the eighteenth century to his own immense erudition, and to the reanimation of the past, he gave a breadth and subtlety to the ideas of the Enlightenment which were often missing in the more programmatic statements of the French *philosophes*.

The argument of the essay is that in recent times, philosophy (into which we should also read 'science' in our sense), in triumphing over learning and *belles-lettres*, is in danger of impoverishing itself by the abuse of its victory. In discarding the intellectual rubbish of past centuries, it runs the risk of failing to discriminate, and of rejecting much which mankind could still learn from the study of the past, from the literature of Greece and Rome, and from the heritage of European scholarship. He had a point. In the advanced thought and the polite world of educated writing and conversation of the mid-eighteenth century, the single-minded devotion to learning which had inspired the scholars and antiquaries (in the mildly contemptuous French term, the *érudits*) of the Renaissance and the seventeenth century had come to seem pedantic and even grotesque: narrowing rather than enlarging the mind, filling it with quaint obsessions, with undigested masses of facts and quotations. The depreciation of mere learning and the quoting of authorities had its philosophical rationale, above all in the new, sceptical 'method' of René Descartes. Descartes' attempt, in his famous *Discourse* (*Discours de la Méthode* (1637)), to recast the foundations of knowledge by resolving initially to try to doubt all received opinions whatever, and by subsequently admitting as well grounded only clear and distinct ideas, placed the whole heritage of knowledge under suspicion, or even condemned it outright. Human reason, not inherited knowledge, was sovereign. The clarity and logical connection of ideas were better guides than learning; simplicity and perspicuity recommended a writer's thoughts more than the embellishments of copious quotations and citation of authorities.

In England, in the seventeenth century, a similar shift of emphasis and enthusiasm took place. The new 'natural philosophy', including experimentation, seemed to point the royal road to truth and to the eradication of past errors, while the elegant mathematics in which Newton expressed the order of the universe made it a model for the virtues of clarity and orderliness. Discoveries had been made and methods forged which clearly surpassed the knowledge and achievements of the ancient world. The recovery and exegesis of classical texts, which had been the essential business of scholars for centuries, was cast into the shade; the learned commentator was outdone by the discoverer of new principles of explanation. There remained enough vitality in the older tradition to maintain Latin and Greek literature as the staple of education, and to prompt, in the late seventeenth century, a running debate over the relative merits and achievements of the Ancients and Moderns. But the superiority of the Ancients, for so long taken for granted, could no longer be assumed, and the new doctrine of progress became one of the commonest and most potent of eighteenth-century assumptions, fully shared by Gibbon.

Historical Pyrrhonism

This reappraisal of the relations of past and present could not leave conceptions of history and opinions of the worth of historical knowledge unaltered. The would-be historian had first to overcome an uncomfortable doubt about his own calling. It was a doubt produced partly by the unflattering contrast between the kind of knowledge and degree of certainty obtainable by historians and the fashionable mathematical and experimental models of precise inquiry and generality of conclusions. But it was also produced by the application of critical reason to the conclusions of the historians and antiquaries themselves. This could lead to suspicion not merely of the value of knowing about the past but of the possibility of knowing anything with any reasonable certainty about the past at all. This scepticism, christened 'Historical Pyrrhonism' (after the Greek sophist Pyrrho, who claimed to doubt everything) sometimes, in the late seventeenth century, took extravagant and even absurd forms. Nevertheless, it did express a more critical attitude towards historical sources and thus, in the longer term, a way forward for the writing of history. The recognition, for example, that apparently authoritative documents had been forged was one source of doubt about the grounds of historical knowledge. But such scepticism contained its own antidote. Documents might be forgeries, but they might also be proved to be forgeries; inauthenticity presupposes authenticity. There had been much forgery in the Middle Ages, but one of the triumphs of Renaissance scholarship had been the exposure by Lorenzo Valla of the supposed deed of gift by the Emperor Constantine of the western empire to the pope, the 'Donation of Constantine'. The study of the styles and handwriting of past documents made great strides in the later seventeenth century, particularly in Paris among the scholars of the religious orders. Gibbon made no direct use of these techniques, but he was a beneficiary of their results.

Another source of doubt about the validity of claims to historical knowledge was the bias of historians. The religious controversy that had torn the Christian world at the Reformation and after was a major source of interest in the past. Each side wished to demonstrate from history the errors and corruption of the other. This impulse sometimes made men historians but it also made historians into advocates. Again, however, the defect proved to some extent self-corrective. Mutual critical scrutiny and the desire for unimpeachable proofs was an inducement to more disciplined scholarly methods.

It took some time, however, before the more rigorous standards of historical criticism which were developed in the later seventeenth century were applied directly to the composition of modern, secular, narrative histories, particularly to the history of the ancient world. There the classical historians themselves still held the field, and it seemed implausible that modern scholars, at a much greater distance from the events recounted, and with few documents other than the ancient histories to rely on, could improve on their accounts. All the same, past narrative histories had disadvantages as sources; their versions of events might reflect little more than the bias of the historian. Medals, artefacts, and inscriptions, the province of the antiquary, seemed more reliable. The demand for rigour in the testing of evidence by the scholars of the seventeenth and eighteenth centuries led in the long run to the writing of a more critical and authentic kind of history. But initially, by making the recovery even of simple facts seem an arduous task, it reinforced a tendency for students of the past to be antiquaries, interested in the accumulation of isolated facts and details for their own sake, rather than constructive narrative historians. Hence the antiquary seemed to the *philosophe* to spend his life in the pursuit of ends which were both doubtfully attainable and in the end not worth attaining: a devotion to compiling

21

useless facts, as the utilitarian philosopher Helvétius said, about barbaric times.

Philosophic history

The remedy, for the apostles of the Enlightenment who continued to believe in the value of history, could be found in the concept of progress itself. The past could be used to illustrate, to celebrate and perhaps even to explain, the course of 'improvement', the development of 'civilization' —a new word of the later eighteenth century. To do this, the study of history must go beyond the record of reigns and battles, of great actions and exemplary lives which had been the staple of classical and Renaissance historiography. It must concern itself, as the ancient historians had sometimes done, with 'manners', and with the 'spirit' (or as we might say, 'mentalities' or 'values') of different periods or societies. Such writing need not even be in any recognizable sense historical; the pioneer work, for the eighteenth century, was Montesquieu's *Spirit of the Laws* (1748), to which Gibbon, like other eighteenth-century writers, notably Adam Smith, owed a heavy debt. The diversity of human societies, which not only history but the European explorations and colonizing enterprises from the sixteenth-century onwards had increasingly revealed, could be described, and the coherence of their ideas and ways of life made intelligible. Written in this way, history could be brought into the 'philosophic' camp and put to work in the service of Enlightenment. Voltaire, for example, wrote his *Essay on Customs* (*Essai sur les Moeurs*, 1756) in order to convince his mistress Mme du Châtelet that history could be instructive.

Gibbon was to play a distinguished part here; his chapters on barbarian manners were to be notable examples of the eighteenth-century interest in ethnography, and the protagonist of the *Decline and Fall* is in a sense not so much Rome as civilization itself. His early speculations on primitive and pagan religious beliefs in the *Study of Literature* were by no means original, but they were indications of what was to come. But Gibbon was critical of over-schematic, over-simplified versions of 'philosophic history', as presented by Voltaire, and sometimes critical even of Montesquieu also, for sacrificing scholarship to theory; the footnotes to the *Decline and Fall* bear this out. To him 'In his way, Voltaire was a bigot, an intolerant bigot' (7.139 n.15). Though Gibbon fully shared the preoccupation of his age with 'civilization' and 'manners', greatly to the enrichment of the *Decline and Fall*, and though he accepted any opportunity to celebrate 'improvement', he remained, and was proud to remain, also a scholar in the more traditional sense. His youthful essay attempted, among other things, to define the vocation of the historian, especially when qualified by the adjective 'philosophic'. Montesquieu was one model for the philosophic historian who seeks the underlying causes of events, but another was a more venerable example, the Roman historian Tacitus. 'Tacitus employs the force of rhetoric only to display the connection between the links that form the chain of historical events, and to instruct the reader by sensible and profound reflections' (L 108).

Philosophic history, then, reveals connections and penetrates below the surface appearance of things to explain their occurrence. History so treated is the pathology of the human mind in action: it is the history of error, prejudice and illusion that chiefly interests the philosophic inquirer, and in his essay Gibbon sketches, with some obvious indebtedness to Hume's *Natural History of Religion* (1757), a possible essay on the origins of polytheism. It was a common eighteenth-century interest. The confidence of the followers of Descartes and Newton in established, rational procedures for the discovery of truth and the rejection of error threw into sharp relief the apparently irrational beliefs adopted without such authorization: they were summed up as 'superstition' and 'prejudice'—two key words for the eighteenth-century Enlightenment. A consciously enlightened mind approached the varieties of magical and religious belief with a cultivated curiosity. Since they were by definition not arrived at by observation or rational inference, their very existence, though omnipresent, became a problem, and the understanding of their pathology an important task. It is in the light of this that we should read the quite common eighteenth-century reflections on the nature of human history which regard it, to quote Gibbon's famous formulation, as 'little more than the register of crimes, follies and misfortunes of mankind' (1.77). This might be so, but it made the task of understanding it only the more urgent.

Antiquaries and historians

But in singling out the young Gibbon's call for 'philosophic history' and his endorsement of eighteenth-century notions of useful knowledge, even with the example of Tacitus as well as Montesquieu held before us, we run some risk of making him into too much of a *philosophe* himself. He certainly knew the intellectual world of the *philosophes*, and his early encounter with Catholicism gave him a sympathy with continental anti-clericalism which few, if any, of his English contemporaries felt so keenly, even though he himself was shocked by the atheism of the Paris salons. And though he defended scholarship against its detractors, he had no ambition to be merely a laborious antiquarian pedant. As he wrote in his journal, in the same year as he published the essay, 'The part of an historian is as honourable as that of a mere chronicler or compiler of gazettes is contemptible' (W 3.551). But in his approbation of the 'philosophic historian' we must not forget the noun while attending to the adjective. Gibbon understood it in a sense more sympathetic to the antiquary and to the critical establishment of facts than Voltaire—to Gibbon's irritation—would have done. It is characteristic of him that he turned his argument for an understanding of underlying historical causes also into one for the establishment of historical facts, even apparently trivial ones. Rejecting the view that only obviously 'useful' facts are valuable, while the rest may be discarded, he went on: 'No, let us carefully preserve every historical fact. A Montesquieu may discover, in the most trivial, connections unknown to the vulgar' (S 110).

By inclination and early pursuits, Gibbon was first an antiquary and a lover of history. His sense of vocation as an historian was enhanced and disciplined by a sense of what it was to be a 'philosophic historian', but it was not created by it. He never worked in archives, but neither did he indulge in instructive or polemical historical essays in the manner of Voltaire. His *Memoir*, the records of his reading in his journals, his occasional writings, and the notes to the *Decline and Fall*, all demonstrate not only his command of antiquarian detail, but his love of it. It laid the foundations of his historical writing, and it also made the element of didactic enlightenment in it all the more formidable. When, in the *Decline and Fall*, he sometimes complains of the tedium of his materials, or even, more rarely, affects a Voltairean disdain—'I am ignorant, and I am careless, of the blind mythology of the barbarians' (5.327)—the reader experiences almost a feeling of shock. Gibbon gaily inflicts it with a teasing sense that he has earned the right to do so by the immensity and minuteness of his diligence. The *Decline and Fall* grew out of Gibbon's antiquarian interests, not the other way round.

Amid the chaotically varied reading of his boyhood—the classical authors, the contemporary 'universal histories', the miscellaneous works of travel and theological disputation—Gibbon himself saw, in retrospect, the first striving for order and discipline in his precocious interest in chronology and geography, 'an early and rational attention to the order of time and place' (M 43). Chronology was an important tool and a matter of concern in seventeenth- and eighteenth-century historiography because it offered the possibility of checking the records of classical antiquity and of the Hebrew scripture against each other and of producing a synthetic account of ancient history. It was also crucial in detecting forgeries through their anachronisms. The young Gibbon took an eager interest in such questions: 'The Dynasties of Assyria and Egypt were my top and cricket-ball: and my sleep has been disturbed by the difficulty of reconciling the Septuagint with the Hebrew computation' (M 43). In the footnotes to the *Decline and Fall* Gibbon was always quick to pounce on errors in matters of dating or to question their authenticity, as well as to denounce geographical inaccuracies. An interest in artefacts, coins, medals, inscriptions, weights and measures, all subjects of close attention by eighteenth-century antiquaries, followed naturally. Gibbon was a devoted reader of the Memoirs of the Academy of Inscriptions and resented the fact that it did not enjoy parity of esteem with the other royal learned societies of Paris (M 99).

These were the raw materials of history, and Gibbon

enjoyed and prized them, but he aspired to be an historian, not an antiquary. For confidence in the possibility of discovering historical truth in written sources, through the application of a rigorous critical method, he was largely indebted to Pierre Bayle's *Historical and Critical Dictionary* (1696). This was one of the most influential works of the late seventeenth century, and it was the product of what Gibbon called Bayle's 'wonderful power . . . of assembling doubts and objections' (M 65). Bayle, impressed above all by the difficulty of ascertaining authentic historical facts, pursued them for their own sake. His work was an historical dictionary or encyclopedia in which the evidence for and against each view of each topic was marshalled and scrutinized. He was not a narrative historian.

For usable, well-established sequential history, arranged in the old-fashioned form of annals, Gibbon went, for the early Christian centuries, above all to the French monastic scholars of the seventeenth century. But for models for the writing of historical narrative, apart from Tacitus, he turned not to France but to the Scotland of his own day, and to the examples of David Hume's *History of England* (1754–62) and the *History of Scotland* (1759) by William Robertson. These were works of impressive narrative organization on a large scale, written not with the unimaginative pedantry of the antiquarian scholar but with the ease and polish of a man of the world and of his own times, writing to be widely read by his contemporaries. Gibbon's admiration for them was unbounded, while they, in turn, were cordially encouraging to him. Not the least of posterity's debts to Hume is his advice to Gibbon to write in English and not in French. Of their congratulations on the publication of the first volume of the *Decline and Fall*, Gibbon wrote, 'The candour of Dr Robertson embraced his disciple: a letter from Mr Hume overpaid the labour of ten years; but I have never presumed to accept a place in the triumvirate of British historians' (M 158). Of the impression their works made on him in the days of his apprenticeship he said: 'The perfect composition, the nervous language, the well-turned periods of Dr Robertson inflamed me to the ambitious hope, that I might one day tread in his footsteps; the calm philosophy, the careless inimitable beauties of his friend and rival often forced me to close the volume, with a mixed sensation of delight and despair' (M 99).

The approach to the Decline and Fall

But Gibbon, sure of his vocation, still had to find a subject. The various projects he toyed with or commenced are all, in marked contrast to the usual experience of authors, far less ambitious than the one he actually successfully undertook. His journal for the early 1760s shows him considering, at different times, various possibilities: the invasion of Italy by Charles VIII of France, Richard I and the Crusades, the Barons' Wars, the Black Prince, Henry V, Sir Walter Raleigh, Sir Philip Sidney, the Marquis of Montrose, the history of Florence. He did some work on Raleigh, only to give up, feeling that he had nothing new to contribute. But the project which chiefly engaged his attention for a number of years, and on which he actually wrote a draft of some length, unpublished during his lifetime, was a *History of the Liberty of the Swiss*, a celebration of their heroic struggle for independence in the later Middle Ages. It was this draft, written in French, which occasioned Hume's letter recommending English. One difficulty was that Gibbon was unable to read German and was forced to rely on his friend Deyverdun for translations. Doubtful of its success, Gibbon arranged for his draft to be discussed at a gathering where he was not known to be the author. The criticisms he heard finally killed the project; Gibbon says he 'delivered my imperfect sheets to the flames' (M 142). In fact the manuscript survived and was posthumously published by Lord Sheffield, and nothing in it suggests that the critics or Gibbon himself were mistaken; the author of the *Decline and Fall* is indiscernible.

Meanwhile, of course, the seed of Gibbon's masterpiece had been, by his own account, sown on his visit to Rome in 1764, though it was not to germinate for some years. The survey of the geography and antiquities of ancient Italy that Gibbon wrote in preparation for his Italian journey constitutes, in a sense, his first unconscious work towards the *Decline and Fall*. In Italy his thoughts were on Rome even before he arrived there. With hindsight, for example, we may see significance in the fact that, as his travel journal records, in the galleries of the Uffizi in Florence his attention seems to have been caught less by the works of the Renaissance than by the portrait busts of Roman emperors. He was already prepared, as his first letter from Rome to his father shows, to regard his visit there as the climactic event of his life. For some years after his return to England, he continued to think of himself as the historian of the Swiss Republics, but in 1768, with that dream over, he began in earnest the awesome task which the ruins of the Capitol and the triumph of the friars over Jupiter had helped to focus. Initially he conceived it merely as the history of the city of Rome, and only later broadened his conception to its full, extraordinary scope and its still more extraordinary fulfilment. In retrospect it was to fill even Gibbon himself with wonder: 'I look back with amazement on the road which I have travelled, but which I should never have entered had I been previously apprized of its length' (L 111.107).

But in 1768 years of preparation as well as writing lay ahead, interrupted by the hours of mute, inglorious servitude on the back-benches of the House of Commons in the parliamentary army of Lord North, then engaged in losing an empire. Gibbon, with his usual sunniness and in the calm, retrospective glow of his own achievement, claimed later to think that his inconspicuous parliamentary career in the years of the American Revolution had not been useless to the historian of the Roman empire: 'the eight sessions that I sat in Parliament were a school of civil prudence, the first and most essential virtue of an historian' (M 156). Despite the distractions of Parliament and of life in London, Gibbon continued to assemble the materials of the monument he proposed to build:

> I insensibly plunged into the Ocean of the Augustan history, and in the descending series I investigated, with my pen almost always in my hand, the original records, both Greek and Latin, from Dion Cassius to Ammianus Marcellinus, from the reign of Trajan to the last age of the western Caesars. The subsidiary rays of Medals and inscriptions, of Geography and Chronology were all thrown on their proper objects: and I applied the collections of Tillemont, whose inimitable accuracy almost assumes the character of Genius, to fix and arrange within my reach the loose and scattered atoms of historical information. Through the darkness of the middle ages I explored my way in the Annals and Antiquities of Italy of the learned Muratori . . . till I almost grasped the ruins of Rome in the fourteenth century, without suspecting that this final chapter must be by the labour of six quartos and twenty years. (M 146–7)

Gibbon here gives the instructed reader some indication both of his chief debts as a scholar and of the nature and difficulties of his task. His primary sources were the works of the Latin and Greek historians themselves, and these were often partisan, contradictory, confused and fragmentary. Gibbon saw his task as comparing, harmonizing and synthesizing them into a cogent and credible narrative, with the subsidiary help of coins and medals, geography and chronology—the results of the work of the modern antiquaries, the *érudits* he had defended in his early essay.

The difficulties were formidable. The *Historia Augusta*, for example, is a compilation of lives of the emperors, by various anonymous authors, probably of the third and fourth centuries. Gibbon said that it had neither method, accuracy, nor chronology. Other, later Roman historians were more reputable. Dio Cassius, a Greek historian who wrote at the beginning of the third century, was a pro-consul and an eyewitness of events succeeding the reign of Marcus Aurelius, but much of his *Roman History* is lost or survives only in summaries. He and Ammianus Marcellinus were the best of Gibbon's sources for the earliest period. Ammianus was close to the Emperor Julian the Apostate, and much of Gibbon's celebrated portrait of the latter is derived from him; he is also an important source for Christianity in the period, but again, much of his history is lost. Gibbon used numerous other classical historians, picking his way as best he could through malevolence, religious bigotry, prolixity, cloudy rhetoric and panegyric. His complaints in the *Decline and Fall* are frequent and heartfelt; the Byzantine historians were particularly castigated. Occasionally he was able to use written sources other than narrative, such as letters and, most notably, the Theodosian Code, a compilation of the laws of the Roman Empire published in 438 and dealing extensively with matters of taxation. Gibbon was able to buy an edition of it with a commentary. 'I used it (and much I used it),' he wrote, 'as a work of history rather than of jurisprudence . . . a full and capacious repository of the state of the empire in the fourth and fifth centuries' (M 147).

For the earlier period of his work there was little modern precedent for the task Gibbon had undertaken in writing a comprehensive narrative history of the empire. The classical historians were still read and thought of as authoritative; modern scholars supplied their works with learned commentaries rather than trying to emulate or surpass their narratives. For the medieval period this was not so. Medieval chroniclers were not given the same status as the ancient historians, and there was no inhibition about writing original histories of the period. Here therefore Gibbon had important modern precursors, his debts to whom he acknowledged with his customary generosity, above all to the historians of medieval Italy: the *Civil History of Naples* (1723) by Pietro Giannone, and the work of the Venetian Fra Paolo Sarpi (1552–1623). But among modern scholars, those to whom Gibbon owed and acknowledged his most extensive debts were the two mentioned in the passage from the *Memoir* quoted above, Tillemont and Muratori. The *Scriptores* of Ludovico Muratori (1672–1751) is a collection of the works of historians of Italy from the sixth to the fifteenth centuries; his *Antiquitates Italiae* is an immense collection of miscellaneous documents with accompanying critical dissertations, covering every aspect of the life of medieval Italy. Gibbon used both extensively, calling Muratori 'my guide and master in the history of Italy'. His greatest debt of all, however, was to the French Jansenist Le Nain de Tillemont (1637–98). Tillemont's two great works, his ecclesiastical history (*Mémoires pour servir à l'histoire ecclésiastique des six premiers siècles*) and his *History of the Emperors* cover the first six Christian centuries. For this period Tillemont provided a collection and a scholarly criticism of all the major sources for the early history of the Empire, concerning himself indefatigably with questions of dating, authenticity and reliability. Gibbon was duly grateful. But Tillemont, a pious Jansenist priest, was a true seventeenth-century *érudit*, a compiler and annalist, devoted to facts and blinkered in vision, with no aspirations to be a narrative historian. Gibbon, by constant use of his work, developed a kind of posthumous intimacy with him; the frequent footnote references to him in the *Decline and Fall* range from awed respect to amused, almost affectionate, condescension: 'The patient and sure-footed mule of the Alps may be trusted in the most slippery paths' (3.48 n.33). Elsewhere Tillemont is 'an useful scavenger!' (3.153 n.52). Of the Christian accusations of loathsome practices against the Gnostic heretics, 'It would be tedious and disgusting to relate all that succeeding writers have imagined, all that Epiphanius has received, and all that Tillemont has copied' (2.80 n.21). But Gibbon's farewell salute to Tillemont has the warmth of comradeship as well as gratitude: 'and here I must take leave for ever of that incomparable guide, whose bigotry is overbalanced by the merits of erudition, diligence, veracity, and scrupulous minuteness' (5.132 n.81).

These were only a few of the chief sources used by Gibbon in preparation for writing his history: the mountain peaks in immense ranges of erudition, literary and antiquarian, classical and modern, Latin and Greek, medieval, oriental and ethnographic. But he still laboured under practical difficulties. So long as he lived under his father's roof his time was not wholly his own, and the latter's spendthrift habits were always an anxiety. His death, in 1770, was almost certainly a precondition, if not of the commencement, then at least of the completion of the history. Further dissipation of the family fortune would have condemned Gibbon to drudgery for his subsistence in the latter part of his life. Gibbon was not hypocritical about the relief: 'the tears of a son are seldom lasting' (M 150). As it was, it took him two years to settle his affairs, but the reward was what he called 'the first of earthly blessings, independence. I was the absolute master of my hours and actions' (M 154–5). He was also ready to write. He had assembled the building blocks; they still had to be shaped and polished into the rational architecture of 'philosophic history' in the fullest sense. At first Gibbon struggled with the author's primeval chaos:

> At the outset all was dark and doubtful: even the title of the work, the true era of the decline and fall of the Empire, the limits of the Introduction, the division of the chapters, and the order of the narrative; and I was often tempted to cast away the labour of seven years. The style of an author should be the image of his mind: but the choice and command of language is the fruit of exercise: many experiments were made before I could hit the middle tone between a dull chronicle and a rhetorical declamation; three times did I compose the first chapter, and twice the second and third, before I was tolerably satisfied with their effect. In the remainder of the way I advanced with a more equal and easy pace. (M 155–6)

'The historian of the Roman empire' was being born.

The first volume was published on 17 February, 1776. The first printing of 1000 copies was sold out almost immediately; a second edition was called for in June, and a third the following year, and Gibbon was able to write that 'my book was on every table, and almost on every toilette' (M 157). Letters of congratulation came from Hume, Robertson, Horace Walpole, and David Garrick. The Scottish historian Adam Ferguson, himself the author of a history of the Roman Republic, wrote that like Thucydides he had given his countrymen 'a possession in perpetuity' (W 1.499). The completion of the remaining five volumes was to take him another eleven years.

4 Rome

Ruins and their morals

Gibbon originally intended to write no more than the history of the city itself. His conception expanded to include the whole history of the Empire, western and eastern, from the reign of Marcus Aurelius in the second century AD to the fall of Constantinople in the fifteenth. Even so, it may sometimes seem to the reader that the title is misleading, not in its pretensions but in its modesty. It is far more than just a history of the Roman Empire, grandiose though that project was. Gibbon devoted considerable attention, for example, to the rival empire of Persia; he traced the rise of two of the world's great religions, Christianity and Islam; he described the manners of the barbarians who overran the Empire, and recounted the history of the medieval papacy and the Crusades; pursuing the causes of the Mongol irruption into Europe at the time of Genghis Khan (Zingis, in Gibbon's spelling, which will be used henceforth) took him briefly into a consideration of China. But for Gibbon himself it was always the Roman Empire and its fate which gave focus and direction to the whole work. It was this conviction which kept him, in its latter part, toiling at the history of Byzantium, which he found uncongenial and contemptible. He magnificently asserted what he called 'my claim to introduce the nations, the immediate or remote authors of the fall of the Roman empire' (7.1), but he insisted equally proudly on the coherence of the entire work:

Nor will this scope of narrative, the riches and variety of

these materials, be incompatible with the unity of design and composition. As, in his daily prayers, the Musulman of Fez or Delhi still turns his face towards the temple of Mecca, the historian's eye shall be always fixed on the city of Constantinople. The extensive line may embrace the wilds of Arabia and Tartary, but the circle will be ultimately reduced to the decreasing limit of the Roman monarchy. (5.171)

The notion of Rome's fall, the pathology of its internal decay, provided much, though not all, of the 'philosophic' interest of his history, while the physical memorials of its greatness epitomised the pathos and grandeur of his theme. As he wrote in his preliminary survey of the final two volumes, anticipating their conclusion, 'I shall return from the captivity of the new to the ruins of Ancient ROME; and the venerable name, the interesting theme, will shed a ray of glory on the conclusion of my labours' (5.173). The history ended where, according to him, it had begun, in the ruins of the Forum and the Capitol.

In Gibbon's emotional response to the ruins of ancient Rome, as in that of a number of his contemporaries, there was more than a long-standing, indeed classical, cultivation of melancholy meditation on the fall of empires and the triumphs of time. True, the eighteenth century responded to such things with a particular acuteness and self-consciousness; ruins and decay inspired much pictorial and poetic effort. It was the other side of the cultivation of polite sociability, of optimism and the belief in progress, and it became part of an aesthetic theory, that of the 'picturesque', while 'graveyard poetry' became a recognized genre. But Imperial Rome occupied a special place. It was what Troy and Carthage had been for the Romans themselves, the central symbol of vanished power

37

and glory, but with the difference that its physical remains could still be seen, as the heart of the Grand Tour made by educated and wealthy Englishmen: a shrine, as Gibbon said, where 'the footsteps of heroes, the relics, not of superstition, but of empire, are devoutly visited by a new race of pilgrims from the remote, and once savage, countries of the North' (7.324–5).

Gibbon was not the only one to note its ironies: Alexander Pope before him, for example:

> See the cirque falls, the unpillared temple nods,
> Streets paved with heroes, Tiber choked with gods:
> Till Peter's keys some christened Jove adorn,
> And Pan to Moses lends his pagan horn.
>
> (*Dunciad* iii. 106–9)

Rome was history's greatest lesson and warning, deeply undermining any excessively glib or mechanical notions of progress. The moralizing approach to it was an ancient one, stretching back to classical literature itself. Roman satirists and historians, often aristocrats writing under the Empire and nostalgic for the oligarchy of the Republic, had portrayed it in terms of corruption and degeneracy. The early Roman Republic, as presented, for example, in Livy's history, stood as a reproach to modern decadence, servility and luxury: a myth of stern simplicity and virtue and heroic patriotism. Ancient Christian writers too, most notably St Augustine in his *City of God*, had an interest in portraying the Empire as corrupt, to exonerate the Christians from the charge made against them by pagans, that the later disasters of Rome, particularly its sacking by the Goths in 410, were due to the Romans' impiety in rejecting the old gods. In a Christian, providential view of history, such calamities could only be the result of sin.

Greatness and decline

Gibbon was heir to this moralizing tradition, and it left profound marks on his history though it did not, as we shall see, possess it completely; the *Decline and Fall* is too complex to be subsumed under any single formula of decay. But to enforce the awesomeness of the story on the reader, it was first necessary to celebrate what had been lost: the extent, unity and tranquillity of the Empire at its zenith, and it is this that Gibbon presents in his first three chapters. 'In the second century of the Christian era, the empire of Rome comprehended the fairest part of the earth and the most civilized portion of mankind' (1.1) is the book's opening sentence. The Empire we are to contemplate stretched, we are reminded, from the Atlantic Ocean to the Euphrates and the deserts of Arabia and Africa. We have a roll-call of its provinces, each comprising many future nations and states. We are reminded of the discipline of the legions, and of the absolute control of the Mediterranean, which made it a Roman lake; of the peace and prosperity, the uniformity of law and administration, of the religious toleration which assisted the assimilation of previously hostile barbarians into docile provincials, willing participants in Roman civilization.

It is a vision, like Virgil's though more detailed, of Roman peace and greatness; but where Virgil, in the *Aeneid*, made it a vision of an illimitable future, in Gibbon it is already, of course, necessarily touched with the irony of hindsight. The historian, as his survey comes towards an end, begins to draw our attention to the hairline cracks in the great edifice. Later, as the progress of decay begins to become evident, the admiration becomes ironic or nostalgic, as, for example, in the account of the games held in 248 to celebrate the thousand years since the city's presumed foundation:

Since Romulus, with a small band of shepherds and outlaws, fortified himself on the hills near the Tiber, ten centuries had already elapsed. During the first four ages, the Romans, in the laborious school of poverty, had acquired the virtues of war and government: by the vigorous exertion of these virtues, and the assistance of fortune, they had obtained, in the course of the three succeeding centuries, an absolute empire over many countries of Europe, Asia and Africa. The last three hundred years had been consumed in apparent prosperity and internal decline. The nation of soldiers, magistrates, and legislators, who composed the thirty-five tribes of the Roman people, was dissolved into the common mass of mankind, and confounded with the millions of servile provincials, who had received the name, without adopting the spirit, of Romans. A mercenary army, levied among the subjects and barbarians of the frontier, was the only order of men who preserved and abused their independence. By their tumultuary election, a Syrian, a Goth, or an Arab, was exalted to the throne of Rome, and invested with despotic power over the conquests and over the country of the Scipios. (1.193–4)

At the symbolic point of collapse of the Western Empire, with the entry into the city in 410 by a barbarian conqueror, Alaric the Goth, Gibbon again tellingly chooses to remind the reader of the great span of the already venerable city's existence.

At the hour of midnight the Salarian gate was silently opened, and the inhabitants were awakened by the tremendous sound of the Gothic trumpet. Eleven hundred and sixty-three years after the foundation of Rome, the imperial city, which had subdued and

civilized so considerable a part of mankind, was delivered
to the licentious fury of the tribes of Germany and Scythia.
(3.321–2)

It is not merely Rome but civilization that is humiliated as
the Gothic warriors

> insulted the villas and gardens once inhabited by
> Lucullus and Cicero, along the beauteous coast of
> Campagna. Their trembling captives, the sons and
> daughters of Roman senators, presented in goblets of
> gold and gems, large draughts of Falernian wine to the
> haughty victors, who stretched their huge limbs under
> the shade of plane trees . . . (3.332–3)

In its subsequent long decay, the city begins to present
something like its modern character, as Gibbon had seen
it: a Christian city squatting on the ruins of its past. At the
end of the sixth century,

> if chance or necessity directed the steps of a wandering
> stranger, he contemplated with horror the vacancy
> and solitude of the city, and might be tempted to ask,
> where is the senate, and where are the people? . . . The
> edifices of Rome were exposed to the same ruin
> and decay; the mouldering fabrics were easily over-
> thrown by immolations, tempests, and earthquakes;
> and the monks, who had occupied the most advan-
> tageous stations, exulted in their base triumph over the
> ruins of antiquity. (5.32)

The same resonances are called up by the last years of
Byzantium seven hundred years later, with the Roman
Empire shrunk now to the suburbs of Constantinople.
Venice and Genoa contend for the remains of the Empire,
but when the Emperor signs a treaty with the Venetians

'the weight of the Roman empire was scarcely felt in the balance of these opulent and powerful republics' (6.512). Under the rule of the Catholic crusaders, even the church of St Sophia, the greatest monument of the Greek communion, stands empty, deserted by the people, for whom it had been polluted by the celebration of the Latin rite, 'and a vast and gloomy silence prevailed in that venerable dome, which had so often smoked with a cloud of incense, blazed with innumerable lights, and resounded with the voice of prayer and thanksgiving' (7.177). Awe and contempt are held in an artful balance by the modulations of the elegiac tone. Contemplating its final dissolution, Gibbon also celebrates its longevity: 'the entire series of the Roman emperors, from the first of the Caesars to the last of the Constantines, extends above fifteen hundred years: and the term of dominion, unbroken by foreign conquest, surpasses the measure of the ancient monarchies—the Assyrians, the Medes, the successors of Cyrus, or those of Alexander' (5.243). 'Attention to the order of time and place', which had been, for the young Gibbon, the beginnings of intellectual discipline and accuracy, could also be turned to the uses of irony, elegy, and celebration.

Civic virtue and corruption

But though he traced the decline of the Empire, and in some measure, in the opening chapters, and in occasional ironic reminiscences, celebrated its greatness, Gibbon's own allegiance was given to what he called 'the purer ages of the commonwealth' (1.9), the Republic of the Scipios and of Cicero. In appraising the achievements of Imperial Rome, he viewed them with an eye that was critical and already nostalgic. He derived from his reading in the works of the Roman senatorial class, above all perhaps from Cicero and Tacitus, a conception of senatorial gravity and public virtue that inevitably responded disdainfully not only to the bizarre activities of homicidal boy-emperors, but also to the larger changes that inevitably came over the Roman world as the old, oligarchic, conquering city-state expanded into a vast cosmopolitan empire. In the process, the Empire's cultural and political centre of gravity was pulled across the Mediterranean by the older and richer urban civilizations of the East, giving it an oriental religion and the political character of an oriental monarchy. Gibbon was, after all, himself a member of an oligarchic, exclusive but constitutionally free and powerful senate, the eighteenth-century English House of Commons, educated in the Latin orators, historians and satirists. Roman senatorial and eighteenth-century English Augustan and parliamentarian attitudes blended easily—it was not for nothing that the statues of eighteenth-century statesmen sometimes depict them in togas. Gibbon judged the Roman Empire by the standards they gave, and derived from them, in a significant measure, his explanations of its decline.

We might begin, for example, by considering the possible implications of the word 'Augustan', as applied to the state of England in the earlier part of the eighteenth century. The Emperor Augustus, whose unostentatious autocracy had brought an era of peace and prosperity to the Roman world torn by the factions and civil wars of the later Republic, was an obvious and flattering image of the ruler as restorer of harmony and order. Charles II, whose Restoration in 1660 brought an end to the confusions of the period of the English Civil War and the Commonwealth, was a natural candidate for comparison, and had been hailed as such by the royalist poets, notably by John Dryden. Moreover, the taste of the early eighteenth century for expansive grandeur disciplined into elegance and neo-classical correctness found congenial models in the age of Augustus. Politically, however, the

43

Augustan model could be a disturbingly equivocal one. There was, after all, the celebratory image of him presented by Virgil, but there was also the hostile one offered by Tacitus—a tyrant by stealth. The first of the Emperors, nominally only the first citizen of the Republic, had made himself an autocrat under the forms of Republican legality and equality. As Gibbon put it, he chose 'to reign under the venerable names of ancient magistracy, and artfully to collect in his own person the scattered rays of civil jurisdiction' (1.64). In this way he had reduced the senate to virtual impotence, while claiming to be only its instrument. So seen, Augustus provided a precedent for restored peace and order brought to a polity that had been made ungovernable by faction, but only at the price of tyranny and the concealed but permanent subversion of a free and ancient constitution.

Eighteenth-century Englishmen opposed to the government of the day often displayed, either as a genuine political obsession or perhaps more often as a matter of political tactics and rhetoric, what now seems an exaggerated suspicion of executive government, focusing particularly on that of Sir Robert Walpole, and again upon the ministries of the earlier part of the reign of George III, during some of which Gibbon sat as a Member of Parliament. The Revolution of 1688 and its aftermath had made control of the House of Commons absolutely indispensable to the conduct of government, but in the absence of anything like party discipline this could only be achieved by what was called corruption or, more politely, 'influence': a political spoils-system of jobs, sinecures, favours, and emoluments of all kinds. Inevitably, opposition focused on corruption and professed to see in it the threat of despotism under the forms of parliamentary government.

The moral and theoretical grounding of these attacks was provided by two components, whose influence on eighteenth-century political argument has been brought out in recent years by a number of scholars, most notably by J. G. A. Pocock in his book *The Machiavellian Moment*. Both stem ultimately from antiquity, and are filtered into eighteenth-century English political theory and rhetoric through, in particular, Machiavelli's *Discourses on Livy* (1519–21) and James Harrington's *Oceana* (1656). The first component is an exalted conception of public or civic virtue or patriotism, associated particularly with republican forms of polity; the second is the notion which, above all through Harrington, came to have a particular significance in eighteenth-century England: the idea of a balanced or 'mixed' constitution. These, in conjunction, came to be taken, in the rhetoric of parliamentary opposition, as the indispensable elements and guarantees of political freedom.

Freedom required civic virtue in its citizens both for external defence and for internal vigilance. Such active political virtue or patriotism held in check both foreign enemies and the ambitions of any one faction in the state. A special and sinister role was reserved among threats to liberty for the concept of corruption by the growth of 'luxury'. Civic virtue was constantly liable to be subverted by it; citizens were seduced from active participation in public life by the enjoyment of private affluence, becoming the acquiescent subjects or even the willing tools—'slaves' in the robust eighteenth-century term often used in this sense by Gibbon—of a despotic ruler. In the same way liberty can be lost to an external conqueror when luxury subverts the military as well as the political virtues. The corruption of an energetic, patriotic people by luxury was thought to operate as a kind of entropy, slackening the taut political nerve of public virtue. Energy, virtue and freedom were set in standing opposition, in a way that every reader of the *Decline and Fall* will recognize, to 'enervation', luxury and despotism. It was an opposition which, for the eighteenth century, sometimes rendered the idea of progress, as the development of peace, 'opulence' and 'refinement', an equivocal one, and gave an edge of anxiety to its own conscious enjoyment of these benefits of civilization. It was this which, above all, constituted the awful lesson of Roman history, as a correlative for contemporary English political anxieties and animosities.

As a political creed the extremer versions of the 'patriotic' rhetoric of political virtue, used as the watchword of the radical opposition to executive government, were distasteful to Gibbon. It was this sense that he rejected when he wrote in a letter in 1779, 'I have not any claims to the injurious epithet of a Patriot' (L 2.202). He was, after all, himself a government placeman and supporter of Lord North's ministry, but also temperamentally inclined to moderation and suspicious of too much zeal. Yet for all that, the fundamental concepts of the 'civic virtue' school of political discourse as applied to the example of Rome— and it was, of course, initially derived from the self-criticism, anxieties and nostalgia of the classical writers themselves—provide, as Pocock has also shown, an indispensable key to an understanding of the *Decline and Fall*. It crucially informs Gibbon's diagnosis of the decline of Rome, and, in the slightly looser form of a story of hardy simplicity enervated by luxury and eventually falling into servility and weakness, it occurs as a formula not only for Roman history but for that of the barbarian peoples who acquire and then often forfeit dominion over the provinces of the Empire, successively re-enacting the same drama of conquest, degeneration and ultimate subjection.

Citizens in arms and mercenary armies

Crucial in this latter stage of development, and particularly prominent in Gibbon's account of Rome's decline, is not only despotism and its concomitant, servility, but the employment by an 'enervated' people of mercenary or even foreign troops to defend it. The active and patriotic citizen-soldier who sinks into the enjoyment of private affluence, just as he readily resigns the task of government to a despot, also makes over his own military duties to hired professionals. This strain in Gibbon's thinking is evident in the treatment of a key element in his account of Rome's decline, the Roman army. One of the fundamental polarities presented in the Machiavellian complex of ideas centring on the concept of republican civic virtue was that between a citizen militia and a mercenary standing army. A professed enthusiasm for the idea of a citizen militia and dislike and suspicion of a standing army as both dangerous to freedom and a drain, through taxation levied on land, on the incomes of the country gentlemen, became a favourite theme of the rhetoric of opposition in eighteenth-century England. The militia, to which Gibbon rather reluctantly gave two years of his life, was, as he says, not merely a measure of defence but a patriotic and constitutionalist shibboleth.

The expansion of the Empire and the growing reluctance of citizens to serve permanently in distant frontier camps led inevitably to the degeneration of the Roman legions, from the *beau idéal* of a patriotic citizen army, into a dangerous body of hired barbarians. This forms the central theme of the earlier part of Gibbon's history. As the indispensable agent of despotism, the army, no longer representative of Rome and retaining no traces of republican virtue or sentiment, but representing only its own mercenary interests and *esprit de corps*, became the ultimate arbiter of a state in which it was an alien body. After the preliminary survey of Gibbon's first three chapters, the next ten form a distinct section. It is a story whose protagonist is the Emperor's Pretorian Guard, stationed permanently in Rome as the despot's own military force, by which he overawes the senate, but by which he is himself overawed and often murdered; his successor is elected by the whim of the soldiers or by the latter selling the imperial title to the highest bidder, who becomes in turn, in Gibbon's phrase, 'the imperial slave'. When the legions in the provinces attempt to join in the profitable game of emperor-making, the Roman world is torn by military civil wars.

From European republic to oriental despotism

The fractiousness of the army is eventually tamed by the strong autocracy of Diocletian and Constantine in the late third and early fourth centuries, but at a heavy cost. The seat of government is removed from Rome, at first spontaneously, following the military despot on his campaigns, and finally, deliberately, to the new city of Constantinople. This transition is both cause and consequence of the confirmation of despotism and of the barbarizing and orientalizing of the Empire. The Emperors, sprung from and created by a mercenary army of Romanized barbarians, are not Romans or even Italians, and have no feeling for the—essentially republican— traditions of the city, such as was possessed even by the first Caesars. Roman citizenship itself, once a jealously cherished privilege, is increasingly extended to the provincials, who, again, have no heritage of republican tradition, while the old capital itself sucks in the floating population of the Empire. As Rome ceases to be the political centre of the Empire, the authority of the senate and consuls, already reduced virtually to nullity by the successors of Augustus, dwindles further into an archaic ritual. In Constantinople the ritual vestiges of republican freedom take their place amid the courtly ceremonial of an oriental despot. 'By the philosophic observer, the system of the Roman government might have been mistaken for a splendid theatre, filled with players of every character and degree, who repeated the language and imitated the passions of their original model' (2.160).

This transformation is only the most politically important aspect of a wider process, begun as the corruption of the austere high culture of the Roman aristocrats of the Republic and early Empire by a flamboyant orientalism, which, for Gibbon, is the extreme of degeneracy. Christianity, which will be considered in the next section, is an aspect of this orientalization, but the outward signs among the Roman upper class appear early, in the adoption of oriental cosmetics, curled hair and the elaborate eastern insignia of royalty, increasingly favoured by the Emperors, all contemptuously comprehended by Gibbon as 'effeminacy' and 'the luxury of Asia'. The political terminus of this process replaces haughty and dignified republicans and aristocrats by powerful but servile court officials of mean origin:

> The manly pride of the Romans, content with substantial power, had left to the vanity of the East the forms and ceremonies of ostentatious greatness. But when they lost even the semblance of those virtues which were derived from their ancient freedom, the simplicity of Roman manners was insensibly corrupted by the stately affectation of the courts of Asia. The distinctions of personal merit and influence, so conspicuous in a republic, so feeble and obscure under

a monarchy, were abolished by the despotism of the emperors; who substituted in their room a severe subordination of rank and office, from the titled slaves who were seated on the steps of the throne, to the meanest instruments of arbitrary power. (2.159)

In Gibbon's reiterated references to 'the indolent luxury of Asia' and similar phrases, there is often an implied climatic determinism or something like it, perhaps inherited from Montesquieu's *Spirit of the Laws*; it is never fully elaborated, but often referred to: the stretched nerve of civic and military virtue is relaxed in the 'softness' of a warm climate. There was a cultural lack of sympathy with Byzantium too, characteristic of his age. The only great Byzantine building Gibbon knew was St Mark's cathedral in Venice, and he described St Mark's Square as 'the worst architecture I ever yet saw' (L 1.143).

Above all, Byzantium stood as the representative of a category of eighteenth-century social and political theory, distinguished by Montesquieu as a distinct political type, to be set alongside monarchies and republics: 'oriental despotism'. The latter stood as the antithesis of the 'mixed' polities, which could vary from republics like Venice or ancient Rome to a constitutional monarchy like England's, to which the eighteenth century's approval was most freely given. Mixed constitutions embodied the idea of constitutional liberty and were most likely to guarantee the private liberty and independence of the subject. The oriental despotism, by contrast, was a levelling regime, reducing all subjects, whatever their wealth or rank, to the same condition of servile dependence on the absolute will of the autocrat. The central political aspect of Rome's decline was the mutation of the one into the other, epitomized in the shift from West to East. In that transition, the itinerant soldier-emperors of the third century were the crucial middle term, and they themselves were the product of the refusal of the native Roman citizen to bear the burden of military service on the now remote frontiers of the Empire. It was in this sense that Gibbon's formula applied: 'the decline of Rome was the natural and inevitable effect of immoderate greatness' (in the chapter subsection entitled 'General Observations on the Fall of the Roman Empire in the West' (4.161)).

In this formula Gibbon followed Montesquieu's argument, in his essay *Considerations on the Greatness and Decadence of the Romans* (1734). But there was another aspect of Gibbon's dislike of Byzantium, and another alleged cause of Rome's decline to which he gave prominence: Christianity. By teaching men to care primarily for their own souls, Christianity turned them away from the practice of the civic and military virtues, and taught them to prefer the discipline of the monastery to that of the legion. In Byzantium, submission to absolute power was matched and fostered, in Gibbon's view, by the abject intellectual servility of superstition. In giving Christianity a significant role in Rome's fall, Gibbon had been preceded, not this time by Montesquieu, but by Voltaire in his *Essay on Customs* and by the French *Encyclopédie*. Nevertheless, the classic 'philosophic' account of the rise of Christianity was Gibbon's. It was, in his day and for long after, the most controversial aspect of *The Decline and Fall*, and the one to which we must now turn.

5 Christianity

Superstition and enthusiasm

An important factor of the peace of the Roman world in the second century, presented at the opening of Gibbon's history, is religious toleration. Antique paganism is eclectic, tolerant, flexible and, to use a favourite word of Gibbon's in such contexts, 'mild'. Its impressive rituals and festivals and graceful individual acts of devotion give coherence, dignity, and reassurance to public and private life; they do not seek to transform it or to transcend its boundaries. The official cults, centred on the figures of the Olympic pantheon and focusing local and civic piety, comfortably accommodate different attitudes to them, different kinds and intensities of recognition and reverence, anxious petition or polite acknowledgement: 'the various modes of worship which prevailed in the Roman world were considered by the people as equally true; by the philosopher as equally false; and by the magistrate as equally useful' (1.28). Faith was promiscuous and scepticism urbane:

> In their writings and conversation the philosphers of antiquity asserted the independent dignity of reason; but they resigned their actions to the commands of law and custom. Viewing with a smile of pity and indulgence the various errors of the vulgar, they diligently practised the ceremonies of their fathers, devoutly frequented the temples of the gods; and, sometimes condescending to act a part on the theatre of superstition, they concealed the sentiments of an Atheist under the sacerdotal robes. (1.30–1)

Into this venerable, gently assimilative world of established but varied cults and unsystematic but traditionally channelled beliefs, Christianity erupted as an alien and destructive force: intolerant, exclusive, dogmatically theological and fiercely zealous, tightly organized, ascetic and contemptuous of the world around it. Gibbon's attitude to the transformation this wrought, like his attitude to the 'barbarizing' of the Roman army and the orientalizing of the Roman polity, was conservative. It was a conservatism shaped by eighteenth-century notions of reason, tolerance and moderation, and above all by the characteristic distaste and suspicion of the high culture of his age towards 'enthusiasm', a word which then carried strong suggestions of fanaticism. 'Enthusiasm', though proselytizing and dangerously contagious, was essentially antisocial, defying established ways and the more cautious approaches to conviction offered by reason and experience. The enthusiast relied solely and uncritically on an inner light of personal certainty, of which he needed no other proof and to whose illumination he recognized no limits. As Hume wrote in his essay 'Of Superstition and Enthusiasm', to which Gibbon refers admiringly,

> In a little time, the inspired person comes to regard himself as a distinguished favourite of the Divinity, and when this phrensy once takes place, which is the summit of enthusiasm, every whimsey is consecrated; human reason, and even morality, are rejected as fallacious guides; and the fanatic madman delivers himself over, blindly and without reserve, to the supposed illapses of the Spirit, and to inspiration from above.

Hume's essay rests on an already well-established

contrast between enthusiasm and superstition. Whereas enthusiasm springs from presumption, the root of superstition is fear. Superstition is therefore favourable to the authority of church establishments and priest-hoods, while enthusiasm is dangerous to them. In this short essay there is the intellectual basis for a reading of the history of religion (though Hume does not draw it out so far) in terms of an oscillation between priestly hierarchies administering established rituals and pro-mulgating authorized doctrines, and inspired, prophetic religious movements, as well as for the interpretation of an obvious contract between Catholicism and Protes-tantism.

The eighteenth-century philosophers' attitudes to superstition and enthusiasm tended to vary accordingly. In their contempt for (though also curiosity about) superstition, there was an implicit contrast between facile credulity, an impulsive leaping to feared or desired conclusions, and the disciplined inquiries of logic, critical history, and physical demonstration. It is indeed only the existence of the latter which gives meaning to the concept of superstition; superstitions are the heresies of an enlightened age. But in the eighteenth-century's attitude to enthusiasm there was more than contempt; there was also a kind of fear. The two preceding centuries had been made bloody and fratricidal by ferocious religious civil wars and civil persecutions. The fabric of society had been shaken and countless lives sacrificed in the strife between Catholics and Protestants. In Protestant England, the Church Establishment had been challenged, often roughly, by self-taught artisans, lay theologians claiming unique possession of religious revelation and a monopoly of truth in the interpretation of Scripture. In eighteenth-century writers, including Gibbon, we often hear a note of self-congratulation on the age in which they live. Its source is not only a belief in progress and science, it is also relief: a profound gratitude for the dawn of a polite and enlightened age which had left behind uncontrolled fanaticism and bigotry, religious civil war and what Gibbon called 'pious murders'.

It was with sympathies conditioned by this gratitude, which was itself tempered with an uneasy awareness of the vast, destructive potentialities of rampant enthusiasm, that Gibbon viewed the advancing Christians of the first centuries—viewed them, as it were, though the eyes of a cultivated, pagan Roman gentleman, fully aware of the vast gulf between his own gentle scepticism and the superstitions of the vulgar. The tolerance characteristic of paganism allowed an equipoise, expressed as a harmonious outward solidity, between these two sharply contrasting intellectual worlds. Christianity upset the balance: in it, superstition was armed with the weapons of intolerance by enthusiasm or zeal, while intellect, subverted by the same fanatical zeal, was prostituted, in theological speculation and controversy, to the service of superstition. Theological animosity had been utterly alien to the religious eclecticism, educated and uneducated alike, of the pagan world. Even the populace could be said to have possessed, if unselfconsciously, something of that cosmopolitanism and freedom from prejudice and bigotry which, in the eighteenth century, was a proclaimed and consciously cultivated virtue: 'Such was the mild spirit of antiquity, that the nations were less attentive to the difference than to the resemblance of their religious worship. The Greek, the Roman, and the Barbarian, as they met before their respective altars, easily persuaded themselves that, under various names and with various ceremonies, they adored the same deities' (1.29).

Gibbon

The society of mankind, and the refinement of orthodoxy

Gibbon shared with the 'enlightened' thinkers of his time a combination of attitudes that was, at least superficially, paradoxical: contempt for the superstitions of the vulgar and a confidence in the general moral sense, the consensus, of mankind. The early Christians often seemed to him both to embody superstition at its most abject, and wilfully to defy the moral consensus of humanity and the values embodied in human society. Often, in his accounts of its bigotry and asceticism, its excesses are contrasted with a universal moral sentiment, 'the pity and indignation of mankind'. Christian exclusiveness and bigotry, and above all monasticism, seemed to him a rejection of society itself. 'The great society of mankind' (2.335) is set in opposition to the selfish absurdity of the anchorites 'who indulged their unsocial, independent fanaticism' (4.72); 'unsocial' carries, in Gibbon, as often in the eighteenth century, a heavy weight of disapproval. It is applied, at the outset of his account of the origins of Christianity in the notorious fifteenth and sixteenth chapters of the *Decline and Fall*, to the Jews, from whom he thinks the Christians derived their intolerant exclusiveness: 'A single people refused to join in the common intercourse of mankind . . . The sullen obstinacy with which they maintained their peculiar rites and unsocial manners seemed to mark them out a distinct species of mankind' (2.2–3). The Christians' similar rejection of the outward conformities of the public life of the Roman world, and the tightknit Christian communities, gave them, when combined with evangelical zeal, a decisive advantage over the easygoing eclecticism of the pagans. Though it drew persecution upon them, it also did much to ensure their eventual victory.

But the spirit of bigotry and exclusiveness also turned inwards, breaking the Christian world, once established, into irreconcilable warring sects: Donatists, Nestorians, Arians, Monophysites, Catholics, and many more. There was nothing perfunctory about Gibbon's treatment of early Christian theology and of the niceties of the metaphysical points, above all the relations of the Father and the Son, and the exact relation of Christ's divine to his human nature, which tore apart the Christian world. As a boy, he had plunged voluntarily into the literature of theological controversy; now he used it with a purpose that was both erudite and satirical. Sectarian exclusiveness becomes not merely destructive but absurd, like the conflict of Big- and Little-Enders in Swift's *Gulliver's Travels*. The Donatists 'boldly excommunicated the rest of mankind' and 'Even the imperceptible sect of the Rogatians could affirm without a blush, that when Christ should descend to judge the earth, he would find his true religion preserved only in a few nameless villages of the Caesarean Mauretania' (2.334–5).

The refinements of Christian theology, and the significance so fiercely and sometimes atrociously attached to them, are constantly set by Gibbon against practical and moral good sense, and in terms which make them seem not merely futile or dreadful, but parochial. The doctrine of damnation is an example:

> The condemnation of the wisest and most virtuous of the pagans, on account of their ignorance or disbelief of the divine truth, seems to offend the reason and the humanity of the present age. But the primitive church, whose faith was of a much firmer consistence, delivered over, without hesitation, to external torture, the far greater part of the human species. (1.26)

Sometimes the judgement is conveyed in the form of ironic compliment:

> In the name of the fourth general council, the Christ in one person, but *in* two natures, was announced to the Catholic world: an invisible line was drawn between the heresy of Apollinaris and the faith of St Cyril: and the road to paradise, a bridge as sharp as a razor, was suspended over the abyss by the master-hand of the theological artist. (5.126)

Part of the weight of the judgement, and sometimes the mischief, is carried in the syntax, as in the remark on the Emperor Constantine, where the contrast is reinforced by the solemn, apparently judicious gravity of the balanced antithesis: 'As he gradually advanced in the knowledge of truth, he proportionately declined in the practice of virtue' (2.310). Occasionally the opposition of qualities is made general and fully explicit, as when Christian self-mortification is contrasted with 'those worldly philosophers who, in the conduct of this transitory life, consult only the feelings of nature and the interest of society' (2.34). 'Society', 'nature' and 'mankind' are for Gibbon the touchstones of sense and genuine virtue. The love of pleasure and of action, tempered by reason and moderation, are, he says, the source of all happiness and virtue: 'The insensible and inactive disposition, which should be supposed alike destitute of both, would be rejected by the common consent of mankind, as utterly incapable of procuring happiness to the individual, or any public benefit to the world. But it was not in *this* world that the primitive Christians were desirous of making themselves either agreeable or useful' (2.35).

Gibbon's own explicit statements on religion are consistent with a rational eighteenth-century deism, a belief in the objectivity of moral standards of a loosely utilitarian kind, and a stoic acceptance of mortality. In measuring the extent of his scepticism, we have to balance remarks such as 'our incapacity to form any judgement of the divine economy'—a belief by which he was prepared adversely to judge pagan Platonic philosophers as well as Christian theologians—with the statement, apparently made with full deliberation, that 'The God of nature has written his existence on all his works, and his law in the heart of man' (5.339). He approached superstition and enthusiasm in a spirit of pathological inquiry, and sometimes of indignant irony. But he was, as he admitted in the *Memoir*, taken aback by the vehemence of Christian reaction to his fifteenth and sixteenth chapters, on the rise of Christianity, and he acknowledged that, had he anticipated it, he would have been more cautious. He made a spirited and successful justification of his accuracy as an historian in a separately published *Vindication*.

In the *Memoir*, written in tranquillity years later, he ironically congratulated himself on having been the means of some of his assailants' preferment in the Church of England as the reward of their zeal: 'poor Chelsum was indeed neglected, and I dare not boast of making Dr Watson a bishop; but I enjoyed the pleasure of giving a Royal pension to Mr Davies, and of collating Dr Apthorpe to an Archiepiscopal living' (M 160).

The presuppositions of irony

Gibbon had been incautious; it was perhaps a mark of his 'foreignness' in England, for in Paris he felt a moderate among atheist zealots. Yet he was not altogether wrong in thinking the philosophic cause already more than half won. He may have applied to himself his own remark on Cicero: 'We may be well assured that a writer conversant with the world would never have ventured to expose the gods of his country to public ridicule, had they not already been the objects of secret contempt among the polished and enlightened orders of society' (1.30). A sentence such as 'The laws of nature were frequently suspended for the benefit of the church' (2.69–70) is ironical or not in its effect depending on the beliefs of its readers. The standards of rationality, utility and humanity that underlay Gibbon's ironies, the scepticism or distaste that he demurely insinuated or occasionally proclaimed with vigour, did not differ significantly from those of an intelligent, cultivated and humane eighteenth-century Protestant. Most of his themes—the incredibility of the Church's miracles, the perniciousness of superstition, the lazy, unsocial uselessness of monks, the absurd fanaticism of hermits and ascetics—were long-standing Protestant aversions, to which the eighteenth century was adding its own humanitarian and scientific emphasis. But the ruthless exposure and irreverent mockery of the early Church were unquestionably a matter for concern.

Miracles were a case in point. Protestants, refusing to accept the full Catholic tradition of the church, and regarding the supposed miracles of saints and bishops as the product of Catholic superstition, had always been obliged to adopt a rather nice chronological distinction between the original and authentic, and the later and spurious. Years earlier, in his reading of Conyers Middleton, Gibbon had met this dilemma and temporarily chosen the path of complete acceptance. Now, in the *Decline and Fall*, he visibly enjoyed the believer's predicament. The ironist finds his opportunity in some ambivalence, some normally happily suppressed inconsistency in the minds of his readers. It was from Pascal, Gibbon said, that he 'learned to manage the weapon of grave and temperate irony even on subjects of ecclesiastical solemnity' (M 79), though he could also have gained hints from Bayle. But Pascal's irony, which operates essentially through a tone of complete solemnity and a patience which allows the victim to talk himself into absurdity, is less diversified than Gibbon's. The latter masters the art of sudden, disconcerting yet subtle variations of diction, imagery and cadence, each insinuating its own apparently innocent, but damning, judgement.

The tone is set by the apparently sombre gravity with which the theme of Christianity is introduced: 'The theologian may indulge the pleasing task of describing Religion as she descended from Heaven, arrayed in her native purity. A more melancholy duty is imposed on the historian. He must discover the inevitable mixture of error and corruption which she contracted in a long residence upon earth among a weak and degenerate race of beings' (2.2). The historian-pathologist assumes a soothing bedside manner which sympathizes with the patient, while clicking his tongue at the symptoms. At its most straightforward, the irony consists of apparent endorsement: 'Augustine is a memorable instance of this gradual progress from reason to faith' (2.15 n.38). More tellingly, it is conveyed in the subtle suggestions of a word or phrase, and a perfectly controlled use of understatement or, in this case, bathos: 'In the primitive church, the influence of truth was very powerfully strengthened by an opinion, which, however it may deserve respect for its usefulness and antiquity, has not been found agreeable to experience. It was universally believed that the end of the world, and the kingdom of Heaven, were at hand' (2.23). It is the almost parodic use of the phrase from eighteenth-century philosophical discourse, 'agreeable to experience', which makes the pivot on which the bathos turns.

Centuries of pious Protestant indignation at the iniquities of the medieval clergy are transmuted by Gibbon into burlesque, as in the remark on the activities of John XII in the Vatican, that 'we read with some surprise . . . that his rapes of virgins and widows had deterred the female pilgrims from visiting the tomb of St Peter, lest in the devout act, they should be violated by his successor' (5.298), whose effect derives not only from the double suggestion of the word 'act' and the conflation of the saint and the pope, but also from the gentle understatement of 'some surprise'. The same raised eyebrow is used with devastating effect in the word 'singular' in reference to the famous ascetic who lived for thirty years on top of a pillar: 'the name and genius of Simeon Stylites have been immortalized by the singular invention of an aerial penance' (4.73).

Occasionally, his ironic strokes are metaphorical. The pious self-castration of 'the learned Origen, [who] judged it the most prudent to disarm the tempter' (2.37) is made ludicrous, however, not only by the image, but by the mischievous use of 'prudent', with its suggestions of statesmanlike caution and domestic economy. Elsewhere the work is done by cadence and the apparent indifference to incongruity, as in the exploits of Ladislas, king of Naples: 'Besieging Rome by land and water, he thrice entered the gates as a barbarian conqueror; profaned the altars, violated the virgins, pillaged the merchants, performed his devotions at St Peter's, and left a garrison in the castle of St Angelo' (7.286). Here, the gabble of clauses of the same simple form, and the hurried alliteration, catch perfectly the impression of a busy, conscientious man hastily attending to the obligations of a conqueror and a Catholic. Such use of bathos, and of satirical incongruity, especially where they are casually insinuated into a list, are favourite devices of Augustan satire, as in Pope's 'Or stain her honour, or her new brocade', or Johnson's list of the miseries of scholars in *The Vanity of Human Wishes*: 'Toil, Envy, Want, the Patron, and the Jail'. But no one uses it more frequently or effectively than Gibbon.

Establishments and iconoclasm

Gibbon's treatment of other, non-Christian, religious beliefs—paganism, Zoroastrianism—is sometimes comparably, though more light-heartedly, ironic. But in his account of the final destruction of paganism there is sympathy too, and a fastidious distaste for Christian iconoclastic vandalism, in its onslaughts on 'the ancient fabric of Roman superstition, which was supported by the opinions and habits of eleven hundred years' (3.190). (Elsewhere, when the icons were Christian and their workmanship Byzantine, Gibbon's classical and Protestant prejudices draw him to the other side (see Chapter 49). The monks, wild ascetics from the desert and Gibbon's particular aversion, led the destruction. There is pathos in the death of the gods, helpless before Christian intolerance:

> It was confidently affirmed that, if any impious hand should dare to violate the majesty of the god, the heavens and the earth would instantly return to their original chaos. An intrepid soldier, animated by zeal and armed with a weighty battle-axe, ascended the ladder; and even the Christian multitude expected, with some anxiety, the event of the combat. He aimed a vigorous stroke at the cheek of Serapis; the cheek fell to the ground; the thunder was still silent, and both the heavens and the earth continued to preserve their accustomed order and tranquillity. The victorious soldier repeated his blows; the huge idol was

overthrown, and broken in pieces; and the limbs of
Serapis were ignominiously dragged through the streets
of Alexandria. (3.202)

Gibbon lays stress, with a disapproval which seems as
much Protestant as philosophic, on the ways in which
Christianity, in its victory, took on many of the features
of polytheism: the belief in signs and omens, and the
cult of the saints, which replaces that of the tutelary pagan
deities: 'the victors themselves were insensibly subdued
by the arts of their vanquished rivals' (3.215). But for
all his condemnations of superstition and idolatry,
his rationalism and proud independence of mind, Gibbon, in the contest between religious establishments and
puritan zeal, was sometimes inclined to the former, and
particularly so in the case of paganism. It is possible to
conceive of Gibbon as a free-thinking abbé of the Parisian
salons, or a latitudinarian clergyman-antiquary, enjoying
what he called 'the fat slumbers of the Church' (M 140).
What is not possible is to imagine him as an earnest
evangelical or zealot of any kind, even the philosophic.
Like most of his contemporaries for example, he was
relatively unapppreciative of the creativity of the Middle
Ages: to him it was a period of darkness for the human
mind. But as Christianity shed some of its early zeal and
became an establishment, he could pay an occasional
grudging tribute, as in the case of Gregorian chant in the
services of the church, for example: 'Experience had shown
him the efficacy of these solemn and pompous rites to
soothe the distress, to confirm the faith, to mitigate the
fierceness, and to dispell the dark enthusiasm of the vulgar,
and he readily forgave their tendency to promote the reign
of priesthood and superstition' (5.35–6). In the tension
between enthusiasm and superstition, there was always

something to be said for the latter. Gibbon was bound to approve of the Reformation, but there was still a note of equivocation and anxiety:

> The imitation of paganism was supplied by a pure and spiritual worship of prayer and thanksgiving, the most worthy of man, the least unworthy of the Deity. It only remains to observe whether such sublime simplicity be consistent with popular devotion; whether the vulgar, in the absence of all visible objects, will not be inflamed by enthusiasm or insensibly subside in languor and indifference. (6.126–7)

It is no surprise that Gibbon welcomed Burke's denunciation of the French Revolution; the analogies between the political iconoclasm of the new zealots in Paris, and the swarms of fanatical monks, the Jacobins and sans-culottes of antiquity, who had 'overspread and darkened the face of the Christian world' (2.319) were too close to be missed. 'I have sometimes thought,' Gibbon wrote in his *Memoir* when recording his endorsement of Burke's *Reflections*, 'of writing a dialogue in which Lucian, Erasmus, and Voltaire should mutually acknowledge the danger of exposing an *old* superstition to the contempt of the blind and fanatic multitude'(M 195). Gibbon, like a number of his contemporaries, subscribed to the idea of a 'double truth', for the enlightened and the vulgar. But he was always a believer in moderation, even in 'philosophy'. The Roman Emperor he most admired, Julian the Apostate, had approached too close to enthusiasm in his devotion to philosophy to be unequivocally approved of. He is rebuked not only for his intolerance towards the Christians but because in the philosophic asceticism of his private life he had failed to learn from Aristotle 'that true virtue is placed at an equal distance between the opposite vices' (2.421).

Gibbon

In the fierce single-mindedness of early Christianity, in its boundless promises, uncompromising judgements and intransigent rejection of civic virtues and the religious practices sanctioned by custom in the ancient world, Gibbon saw both the chief causes of its success and a source of division, weakness, and the internal barbarization of the Empire. In the *Decline and Fall* he had, as he said, described 'the triumph of barbarism and religion' (7.308) whose symbol was the barefooted friars in the temple of Jupiter and the sound of their chanting amid the ruins of the Capitol.

6 Barbarism

The transformation of the world

At one point in his narrative of the fall of the Western
Empire and the rise of Christianity, Gibbon introduces the
old legend of the Seven Sleepers, which tells the story of
some Christian youths who, hiding from persecution in the
time of the Emperor Decius in the middle of the third
century, fall into a charmed sleep of nearly two hundred
years, returning eventually to a changed world in which
they are strangers. Gibbon uses this as a device for putting
before the reader the extraordinary transformations the
Empire had undergone in the interval:

> During this period, the seat of government had been
> transported from Rome to a new city on the banks of the
> Thracian Bosphorus; and the abuse of military spirit had
> been suppressed by an artificial system of tame and
> ceremonious servitude. The throne of the persecuting
> Decius was filled by a succession of Christian and
> orthodox princes, who had extirpated the fabulous gods
> of antiquity; and the public devotion of the age was
> impatient to exalt the saints and martyrs of the Catholic
> Church on the altars of Diana and Hercules. The union
> of the Roman Empire was dissolved; its genius was
> humbled in the dust; and armies of unknown Bar-
> barians, issuing from the frozen regions of the North,
> had established their victorious reign over the fairest
> provinces of Europe and Africa. (3.415)

From the serene mistress of the Mediterranean world the
Empire had become a Christian and almost exclusively

67

Near-Eastern one, centred on Constantinople. In the West, in the face of barbarian raids, Rome had become a walled city by the end of the third century. A respite was won by civil and military reorganization under the 'barbarian' soldier-emperors, Diocletian and Constantine, but in 410, Rome, no longer the political heart of the Empire, had been entered and sacked by the Goths. When, a generation later, it was ransomed from destruction at the hands of Attila the Hun, it was neither the emperor nor the senate but Leo, Bishop of Rome, to whom the Romans looked chiefly as their representative. A century after the Gothic army entered the city, the Western Empire was a patchwork of barbarian kingdoms: Visigoths in Spain and southern Gaul, Franks establishing themselves in the North, and in Italy the monarchy of the Ostrogoths.

It was a transformation to challenge any historian's powers of coherent narrative and thematic organization; Gibbon visibly enjoyed his sense of authorial mastery, as he did later when the Arabs and the Turks swept over the Empire in the East. He had long been an avid reader of travel literature, and his imagination responded eagerly to the vast opportunities. He self-consciously took on the role of impresario of the nations, and celebrated the historian's control of immense events: 'the following nations will pass before our eyes, and each will occupy the space to which it may be entitled by greatness or merit, or the degree of connection with the Roman world and the present age. He is the conductor of huge symphonic movements, in which the scale of the events and the virtuosity of the author are matched: 'I shall lead the Arabs to the conquest of Syria, Egypt, and Africa, the provinces of the Roman empire; nor can I check their victorious career till they have overthrown the monarchies of Persia and Spain' (5.172). Geography had been one of his earliest interests too, and the *Decline and Fall* unrolls for its readers a map of Europe, Asia and North Africa in the first fifteen Christian centuries; there was nothing parochial in Gibbon's interests, and he gave the same scrupulous attention, so far as he was able, to the details of Persian or Arabic history as to Roman, and had apparently as vivid a sense of the geographical features of the Near East—where he had never been—as of the familiar geography of ancient Italy.

He had, too, an intense appreciation, which it is tempting to call romantic, of the strange juxtapositions and vicissitudes of the ages of dissolution and reconstruction. In the days of the Empire's tranquillity, the Mediterranean world had been bound together in a stable pattern through generations, by trade, administrative and linguistic uniformity, and the assimilation of the provincials into Graeco-Roman civic life. Now, in the catastrophic upheavals of the successive immigrations, the lootings and the wanderings of peoples, lines of connection across time and place became strange cultural confrontations. The jarring encounters of nomad tribes, and their diversity of languages and leaders, with the rich past of the Roman world, became normal. As Gibbon saw, it is continuities and survivals which are unexpected and moving. Reminders of the past are poignant: the farms of Catullus and Virgil are trampled by Attila's Scythian cavalry as, almost a thousand years later, Crusaders and Turks heedlessly skirmish in Attica. Such references are elegiac and ironic, but sometimes Gibbon seems almost awed by the extraordinariness of his theme and the vicissitudes of fortune, epitomized, for example, in the seven-branched candlestick taken by the Roman army from the temple at Jerusalem, displayed in the triumph of the Emperor Titus and deposited in the temple of Peace in Rome; then, falling into the hands of the Vandals, 'at the end of four hundred years the spoils of Jerusalem were transferred from Rome to Carthage, by a Barbarian who traced his origin from the shores of the Baltic' (4.6).

In the 'shipwreck of nations', the survival of identity, or the traces of it, were a matter sometimes for wonder, sometimes even for pathos: 'In the tempests of the north, which overwhelmed so many names and nations, this little bark of the Lombards still floated on the surface' (4.343). The fate of the Vandals in Africa is more poignant:

> Even in the present age, and in the heart of the Moorish tribes, a curious traveller has discovered the white complexion and long flaxen hair of a northern race . . . Africa had been their empire, it became their prison; nor could they entertain a hope, or even a wish, of returning to the banks of the Elbe, where their brethren, of a spirit less adventurous, still wandered in their native forests. (4.295)

Gibbon did not reserve the note of elegy only for Rome and the relics of classical civilization.

If ironic juxtaposition was one feature of the barbarian wanderings and settlements to which Gibbon's imagination responded, another was their sheer scale, above all in the empires created in a few years first by the Arabs and then by the Tartars under Zinghis Khan and Timur (Tamberlane). In a few generations in the seventh century and early eighth century, the nomads of the Arabian desert had extended their power, religion and language 'from the confines of Tartary and India to the shores of the Atlantic ocean'. The ancient empire of Persia, long the only serious rival to Rome, disappeared. Southern Gaul was invaded, and the Arab advance reached the Loire: 'the vineyards of Gascony and the city of Bordeaux were possessed by the sovereign of Damascus and Samarcand;

and the south of France, from the mouth of the Garonne to that of the Rhône, assumed the manners and religion of Arabia' (6.14). Five centuries later, in the conquests of the Mongols and Tartars, Peking, Delhi and Samarcand, Baghdad and Damascus, Moscow and Cracow, feel the effects of events which 'may be compared with the primitive convulsions of nature', and 'which, from their uncommon magnitude, will interest a philosophic mind in the history of blood' (7.1).

What this means is indicated by the accompanying footnote, which refers us to an earlier chapter, significantly entitled 'The Manners of the Pastoral Nations' (Chapter 26). Gibbon never lost the historian's indispensable attribute of wonder, or a sense that things could have turned out otherwise, as when he imagined the Arab conquests continuing, with the interpretation of the Koran now taught at Oxford—while 'her pulpits might demonstrate to a circumcised people the sanctity and truth of the religion of Mahomet' (6.15). But 'a philosophic mind' looked for explanations beyond the outcome of battles, and the sociological curiosity of the Enlightenment was not content, in describing the 'manners' of alien peoples, with mere random lists such as earlier generations had appreciated, of exotic customs and practices. Gibbon looked for the explanation of the astonishing conquests of the nomad tribes in Europe and Asia in their native way of life; his treatments of this at various points in the *Decline and Fall*, and particularly the general chapter on the manners of the pastoral nations, are eighteenth-century classics of what would now be called ethnography or social anthropology.

The varieties of mankind

Gibbon was fascinated by the peculiar nature of barbarian

societies as well as by their extraordinary achievements. This interest and his manner of pursuing it were characteristic of the eighteenth-century Enlightenment. They owed much not only to the contemplation of history but to the growing awareness, over the previous two and a half centuries, of the intellectual problem constituted by the varieties of mankind and of human society, revealed by European exploration, colonization and conquest in the non-European world. Partly it was a matter of discovery and contact, partly of enlarged and more disciplined and detailed scholarly and intellectual inquiry. As Gibbon proudly wrote, 'how laboriously does the curious spirit of Europe explore the darkest and most distant antiquities!' (5.404 n. 19). For his descriptions of the manners of the barbarians he was indebted, as he acknowledged, to works by contemporary French authors, like de Goguet's *Origins of Laws and Arts* and, more importantly, de Guignes's *History of the Huns*, as he was to the work of seventeenth- and eighteenth-century English and German orientalists for his accounts of the Arabs and of Islam.

But he was indebted to his intellectual milieu not only for information about the relevant varieties of mankind, but for the categories by which to interpret them.

Like other historians in the Enlightenment—Robertson, in his *History of Scotland*, for example—Gibbon was contemptuous of the older, antiquarian approaches to ancient and alien peoples, through attempts to establish their relations by loosely applied etymologies and to trace their genealogies, usually from the sons of Noah or, earlier, from the Trojans. The critical dismissal of such speculations was an aspect of the discrediting of antiquarian learning we considered in an earlier chapter (Chapter 3). As Gibbon wrote, 'The last century abounded with antiquarians of profound learning and easy faith, who by the dim light of legends and traditions and etymologies, conducted the great-grandchildren of Noah from the tower of Babel to the extremities of the globe'. Gibbon himself subscribed instead to the eighteenth-century environmentalist interpretation: 'similar manners will naturally be produced by similar situations' (1.217–31 n. 72). The influence of climate and geography is a notion (perhaps taken initially from Montesquieu, though it was commonplace enough) which frequently recurs in the *Decline and Fall*, but Gibbon, like his contemporaries, held that it was particularly powerful in the case of savages and barbarians, who were closer to an animal state. Cold was conducive to hardihood and warmth to 'softness', though sometimes, as in the Arabian desert, an enforced austerity produced a rigorous, barbarian way of life similar to that of the northern steppes, the icy plains of Scythia. Barbarian manners, in fact, are characterized by their uniformity.

Actually, Gibbon's accounts of the various barbarian peoples with whom he deals are more sharply individualized than his more general declarations might lead one to expect. As always with him, the historian and antiquary is complemented but not superseded by the 'philosopher'. Nevertheless, behind Gibbon's accounts, and forming their general intellectual framework, is a theory, a system of categories, never woodenly deployed but unmistakable and vital, through which the manners and achievements of the barbarians are to be understood.

The stages of society

In recent years scholars have drawn attention to the presence, in the middle and later eighteenth century, of a general historical scheme, sometimes spoken of as the 'four stages theory'. Human societies, in this scheme, can be divided into four socio-economic types or 'stages' in the progress of 'civil society': savagery (hunting and gathering); barbarism (pastoral); feudal (agricultural); and commercial. It is a scheme particularly powerfully deployed by the eighteenth-century Scots, including those by whom Gibbon was chiefly influenced, Adam Smith and Robertson. By means of it, and the general notion of a history or progress of civil society, 'from rudeness to refinement', they were able to replace older, providential and genealogical accounts of the universal history of mankind. They were also enabled to interpret the diversity of human societies in ways which accommodated the Enlightenment's notions, drawn to a large extent from Montesquieu, of *mœurs* (manners or customs) and *esprit* (spirit or, as we might say, values and characteristic motives), as related structures of thought and habit rather than merely as assemblages of isolated traits which the traveller or antiquarian might itemize.

Gibbon does not use the notion of four stages in any overtly schematic way. He was not concerned with mere hunting and gathering savagery, as Robertson was in his *History of America* (1777). Inevitably he touches on feudalism, and, largely under the influence of his friend Adam Smith, the notion of commerce as bound up with civilization is sometimes emphasized, as we shall see in the next section. But in the conception of pastoralism as the way of life characteristic of barbarian peoples, a distinctive social form with its own typical organization, manners and tendencies, Gibbon found the clue by which to understand the fall of the Roman Empire in so far as it was destroyed not just by internal decay but by external agency: 'the original principle of motion was concealed in the remote countries of the North, and the curious observation of the pastoral life of the Scythians, or Tartars will illustrate the latent cause of these destructive emigrations' (3.70–1).

The manners of the pastoral nations

The fundamental cause, in Gibbon's view, is that pastoralists are essentially nomads, and their way of life involves neither continuous industry nor attachment to the soil. He applies this not only to the nomads of the Central Asian steppes but to the Germans, despite the testimony of his chief source for them, Tacitus' *Germania*, that the German villages practised a form of co-operative agriculture: 'The possession and enjoyment of property are the pledges which bind a civilized people to an improved country. But the Germans, who carried with them what they most valued, their arms, their cattle, and their women, cheerfully abandoned the vast silence of their woods for the unbounded hopes of plunder and conquest.' Being nomad pastoralists, the barbarians are inherently mobile and also inherently warlike. They are bound neither to the soil nor to the city by agriculture or industry, nor are their energies and faculties absorbed in productive labour. Barbarian war is the child of indolence and mobility:

> the same barbarians are by turns the most indolent and the most restless of mankind. They delight in sloth, they detest tranquillity. The languid soul, oppressed with its own weight, anxiously required some new and powerful sensation; and war and danger were the only amusements adequate to its fierce temper. The sound that summoned the German to arms was grateful to his ear. It roused him from his uncomfortable lethargy, gave him an active pursuit, and, by strong exercise of the body, and violent emotions of the mind, restored him to a more lively sense of his existence. (1.221, 223)

The barbarian nomads were not only inclined to war, and by their neglect of agriculture prone to famine and tempted to plunder, they were also constantly organized for it, particularly the mounted shepherds of the Asian steppes and deserts. Regular migrations, the herding of cattle and the pastime of hunting, are all analogies to military manoeuvres. Their home is not a fixed locality but the camp, the tribe in motion. The result was a vast instability, constant movement and collision, with far-reaching, unforeseen effects, among immense organized bodies of warrior-shepherds, from the great wall of China to the Danube and the Rhine. Thus it was the pressure of the victorious Huns which impelled the Goths across the Danube and into the heart of the Roman Empire, while it was the impact of the Tartars on the Islamic world which delayed for a time the fate of Constantinople, and the emergence of the Turks which finally sealed it.

The Arabs and Islam

There is a certain awkwardness, not in Gibbon's extended narrative but in a brief summary such as this, in assimilating the case of the Arabs to that of the shepherds of the North. There is much in Gibbon's account which suggests and even requires such an assimilation. The Bedouin of Arabia Deserta are also nomad pastoralists who embark on a career of conquest and settlement and establish their power over vast areas in an astonishingly short time. But the impulse is different: the rise of one of the world's great religions, Islam. In that respect it would be possible to consider Gibbon's treatment of Mahomet and of Islam as a foil to his account of Christianity. But of course the spread of Islam was inextricably connected with the Arab conquests, as they rolled across the eastern and southern flanks of the Roman Empire, just as the Germans and Huns had done in the north. Gibbon's interest in the Arab world was a long-standing one, dating back perhaps to his childhood reading of the Arabian Nights, and reflected in his desire to take up Arabic at Oxford.

His wish was thwarted, and he was forced, as he admitted, sometimes with a little irritation, to rely on secondary sources in English and French. In the case of the German peoples, he had the classical sources, Tacitus and Caesar, and the work of the sixth-century Gothic historian Jordanes (whom Gibbon calls Jornandes), written in Latin. For the peoples further east he used chiefly the work of French scholars and travellers. But to be confined to secondary, European sources for the Islamic world was far heavier deprivation, for the latter had been literate from the beginning. Inevitably Gibbon was sometimes groping in semi-darkness, and was aware of it, though he was the beneficiary of some substantial scholarship. In his treatment of Mahomet himself, moreover, he was stepping into an eighteenth-century debate on which he lacked the equipment to pronounce. He tried to suspend judgement, but obviously in a narrative could not do so altogether: 'At the distance of twelve centuries, I darkly contemplate his shade through a cloud of religious incense' (5.375).

Mahomet was an equivocal figure for the Enlightenment. On the one hand he could be made, with centuries of Christian prejudice to reinforce the portrait, an archetypal religious enthusiast, or alternatively an impostor. On the other hand his rigid monotheism and rejection of idolatry suggested a favourable contrast with Catholic Christianity. In the latter representation he became a figure always attractive to the eighteenth century, a philosophic legislator, leading his people out of superstition and barbarism and endowing them with a code of laws. Gibbon's account contains elements of both views, not altogether, as he recognises, harmoniously combined.

In general, however, it is a favourable though not uncritical portrait: 'the Koran is a glorious testimony to the unity of God', and Islam has not been subject to the same corruptions as Christianity: 'It is not the propagation but the permanency of his religion, that deserves our wonder' (5.339, 394).

Conquest and corruption

But if Islam remained essentially uncorrupted, the power of the Arabs did not. They experienced the same fate as other originally hardy, warlike peoples, including the Romans, enervated by the luxury of the conqueror, losing the virtues and energy by which their conquests had been achieved. Corruption by luxury, the abandonment of the military virtues, cultural and racial dilution and the loss of liberty in the acquisition of the despotic and servile habits of the peoples they enslave, is, in the *Decline and Fall*, the common nemesis of the conquering nations. In the luxury of Baghdad the Arabs lose their military spirit and their liberty, and the caliphs are driven fatally to rely on the mercenary bravery of the Turks for their defence: 'So uniform are the mischiefs of military despotism, that I seem to repeat the story of the Praetorians of Rome' (6.48). But the Baghdad caliphate, aping the monarchy of Persia, is only one instance of an apparently inexorable law. It is the same with the Goths established in Italy and Spain: luxury, despotism, enervation. 'Alaric would have blushed at the sight of his unworthy successor, sustaining on his head a diadem of pearls, encumbered with a flowing robe of gold and silken embroidery, and reclining on a litter or car of ivory, drawn by two white mules' (5.476). In Africa the Vandals seem equally to parody the vices of the declining Roman Empire. Corrupted with silken robes of oriental cut, baths, chariot races and the theatre, they can offer no effective resistance to the armies of the Emperor Justinian. Even the fiercest of the nomads, the Tartars, are not immune to the fatal attraction of Chinese civilization, and the successors of Cublai Khan 'polluted the palace with a crowd of eunuchs, physicians and astrologers' (7.20).

Barbarian and civilized man seem locked in a perpetual, fatal symbiosis, in which the virtues of the former and the vices of the latter are equally destructive to both: 'the successful shepherds of the North have submitted to the confinement of arts, of laws, and of cities; and the introduction of luxury, after destroying the freedom of the people, has undermined the foundations of the throne' (3.79). It is an apparently endless cycle, which points to something profoundly ambiguous in the conception of civilization itself.

7 Civilization

Barbarism and civilization

One of the most characteristic and easily recognizable features of Gibbon's writing is its use of balance and antithesis. It was a favourite Augustan stylistic device. Pope, for example, uses it in lines which encapsulate in advance much of the argument of Gibbon's *Decline and Fall*:

> . . . the same age saw learning fall, and Rome.
> With tyranny, then superstition joined,
> As that the body, this enslaved the mind;
> Much was believed, but little understood,
> And to be dull was construed to be good;
> A second deluge learning thus o'er-run
> And the Monks finished what the Goths begun.
>
> (*Essay on Criticism* ll.687–91)

In Gibbon, as in Pope, the device is a recipe for pointedness and compression: 'the dissatisfied people . . . accused at once his indolent tameness and his excessive severity', or 'She was doomed to weep over the death of one of her sons, and over the life of the other' (1.140, 141). But it is much more than simply a stylistic trick. The argument of the *Decline and Fall*, as we have already partly seen, revolves around a number of fundamental polarities. The decline of Rome is largely conceived in terms of a set of moral antitheses: liberty/servility, vigour/enervation, manliness/effeminacy, simplicity/luxury. Christianity introduces another set: fanaticism/moderation, superstition/reason (or, sometimes, philosophy), theology/ morality, asceticism/nature, unsocial/social. But the most fundamental, though not the most often invoked, of all these oppositions, the one which gives shape to the entire work, and which leads Gibbon at one point to anxious speculation and affirmation about the future ('General Observations', (4, Chapter 38)), is that between barbarism and civilization.

What is, in a sense, the turning point of the *Decline and Fall* is described in terms of this fundamental antithesis:

> This memorable passage [of the Rhine] of the Suevi, the Vandals, the Alani, and the Burgundians, who never afterwards retreated, may be considered as the fall of the Roman empire in the countries beyond the Alps; and the barriers, which had so long separated the savage and the civilized nations of the earth, were from that fatal moment levelled with the ground. (3.269)

The shrinking of the boundaries of civilization to a corrupted remnant, and the beginnings of its revival from a new and firmer basis, provides the overall pattern of Gibbon's history, and it gives a work chiefly devoted to the account of decadence and destruction and entitled 'Decline and Fall', the shape of optimism. Despite Gibbon's reservations about Roman civilization at its height, about its uniformity and lack of vigour and independence, his book, like Milton's epic to which it has been compared, is a story of paradise lost and regained.

The concept of civilization and the progress of society

'Civilization', as we saw earlier (Chapter 3), was a new word of the later eighteenth century, brought originally from France. The sense of the need for such a term derived from the same complex of ideas which produced the notion of the progress of civil society—to which 'civilization' is almost an equivalent—and also the extensive currency of other words derived from the ancient Greek and Roman city or *polis*: 'civil', 'polished', 'polite'. They implied criteria of appraisal for morals and manners—the distinction was sometimes thought too blurred—that were secular and social, and that derived less from chivalry and the aristocratic sense of honour and from courts than from the common life of men in towns; criteria that valued restrained but easy manners and tolerant and agreeable social intercourse. More comprehensively, they suggested a way of judging and comparing whole societies not in religious or constitutional terms, but by the degree of their progress in the arts and sciences and in the improvement of reason, manners and information: from 'rudeness' to 'cultivation' or 'refinement'. The conversations of Johnson and Boswell, as recorded by the latter, often dwell on such comparisons, applied to the rivalry of England and Scotland. They gave content to the idea of improvement, and hence substance to the concept of progress.

Gibbon's celebration of the progress of society and 'the improvement of human reason', and his gratitude at belonging to 'an enlightened age', is a minor but recurring theme in the *Decline and Fall*. He is proud of the achievements of his civilization and his century, and they evoke in him a sense both of wonder and optimism. It is a theme that is more often associated with Macaulay's history a century later, but it is present in Gibbon. The improvement that has taken place in what were the wildest parts of Europe in the days of the Empire justifies our largest hopes for the extension of civilization:

If, in the neighbourhood of the commercial and literary town of Glasgow, a race of cannibals has really existed, we may contemplate, in the period of the Scottish history, the opposite extremes of savage and civilized life. Such reflections tend to enlarge the circle of our ideas: and to encourage the pleasing hope that New Zealand may produce, in some future age, the Hume of the Southern Hemisphere. (3.44)

'The most civilized part of mankind'

Because the concept of civilization transcended the boundaries both of nations and states, it provided the protagonist for an historical story wider than that of the nations, polities, or institutions which still form the chief subjects of history: one could also try to write, as Adam Ferguson did, *A History of Civil Society.* It is to the same body of ideas that Gibbon's remark belongs when he declares that 'a philosopher may be permitted to enlarge his views, and to consider Europe as one great republic, whose various inhabitants have attained almost the same level of politeness and cultivation' ('General Observations', (4.163)). The international republic is not, as it would once have been, 'Christendom', with its antithesis as heathens or the infidel, though it is more or less coextensive with it, but 'civilized society', and its opposite is, as it was for the Greeks and Romans, barbarism. This may seem sufficiently obvious, but it is worth stressing, for it makes the story Gibbon tells more than a merely political one of the downfall of a great empire. To achieve the tragic grandeur with which Gibbon invests its ruin—'the greatest . . . and the most awful scene in the history of mankind'— the Empire must have stood for more than merely power, and its fall must be a catastrophe for mankind, a great hiatus in the course of human improvement. It must have embodied, imperfectly and insecurely yet impressively, the values and achievements of civilization, and Gibbon is at pains, initially, to stress that this was so, and to distinguish the Roman Empire from merely barbarian ones: 'It is not alone by the rapidity or extent of conquest that we should estimate the greatness of Rome . . . But the firm edifice of Roman power was raised and preserved by the wisdom of ages. The obedient provinces of Trajan and the Antonines were united by laws and adorned by arts' (1.28). The larger theme of the *Decline and Fall* is announced in its opening sentence: 'the empire of Rome comprehended . . . the most civilized part of mankind'. Such a view echoed, of course, that of the Romans themselves; it had been inherent in Virgil's celebration of the age of Augustus. His *Aeneid* is the story of the fall of a city, Troy, and its rebirth as Rome. The scope of Gibbon's *Decline and Fall* is wider, but its shape is similar; it ends with the Renaissance.

Of course, it is more than just a rebirth. Gibbon had no wish to reverse the verdict of the battle of the Ancients and Moderns (see above, Chapter 3); he criticized the imitativeness of the Renaissance, and, despite his famous declaration that the age of the Antonines was the one in which a man would have chosen to live, he had no doubt that his own age in most respects surpassed the achievements of the Romans. Rome, for example, was a slave-owning society, and though Gibbon did not dwell greatly on slavery, and drew a distinction between the ancient form and the modern, he left no doubt of his hostility to it. In the encounters of Romans and barbarians, moreover, his point of view is not exclusively that of the former: 'The Romans, who so coolly and so concisely mention the acts of *justice* which were exercised by the legions, reserve their compassion and their eloquence for their own sufferings' (3.116). The Emperor Justinian's reconquest of Italy, which had become a peaceful Gothic kingdom, was wanton and destructive. In his account of the political dealings of Byzantium with the Huns, it is the former which is devious, treacherous and cruel, while the Huns are honest and straightforward. Decadence could be more unattractive than barbarism, which has its own characteristic virtues in the positive aspects of savage independence: courage, honour, personal dignity and hospitality. Barbarian societies have their own principle of vitality and even, up to a point, creativity; their laws are rude but 'adapted to their wants and desires, their occupations and their capacity' (4.123).

Nevertheless, there is only a little of the eighteenth-century primitivist, the sophisticated idealizer of savage virtue, in Gibbon's account of the barbarians; his own allegiance was never really in doubt. Though barbarian freedom, bravery and vigour might sometimes shine brightly when set against the servility and corruption of the later Empire, there was still a vital difference between the regular and rational liberty of constitutional freedom and the 'wild independence' of the barbarian. Barbaric life was indolent, squalid and cruel. The Germans, for example, 'passed their lives in a state of ignorance and poverty which it has pleased some declaimers to dignify with the appellation of virtuous simplicity' (1.218).

In the vices of the corrupted Romans, the unworthy successors of Cicero and Tacitus, Gibbon saw essentially a betrayal of civilization, of reason as well as of civic virtue. He shared the sense of the Renaissance scholars, whose heir he was himself, that classical learning and literature were a precious heritage, the treasury of mankind which had only precariously and imperfectly survived the wreck of Roman civilization itself. With the Renaissance, after the barbarism and ignorance of the Middle Ages, 'The students of the more perfect idioms of Rome and Greece were introduced to a new world of light and science; to the society of the free and polished nations of antiquity; and to

a familiar converse with those immortal men who spoke
the sublime language of eloquence and reason' (7:130).

Civilization and corruption

In the *Decline and Fall*, it is the powerful sense that the
Roman Empire is the trustee of civilization which makes
the initially barely perceptible cracks in the great edifice so
ominous, and also disturbingly ironic because they seem
the inevitable consequences of its grandeur and perhaps,
more disturbingly still, of civilization itself. At the height
of their prosperity, the citizens of the Empire 'enjoyed and
abused the advantages of wealth and luxury' (1.1). The
Greeks had been 'long since civilized and corrupted' (1.38),
a phrase applied with an equally perturbing casualness to
the Persians. As Gibbon traces the decline, the ominous
conjunction begins to seem like an iron law of
degeneration, the nemesis of civilization. In the strenuous,
moralizing tradition of political analysis derived from the
ancient world, above all through Machiavelli's *Discourses*,
of which Gibbon was partly the inheritor, peace and
prosperity are among the greatest dangers to the liberty and,
in the long run, the safety of a state. Thus, in his second
chapter, Gibbon tells us that 'This long peace, and the
uniform government of the Romans, introduced a slow and
secret poison into the vitals of the empire. The minds of
men were gradually reduced to the same level, the fire of
genius was extinguished, and even the military spirit
evaporated' (1.56). Mankind seems locked into a hopeless
paradox in which the enjoyment of the blessings of
civilization is only the precursor of corruption and
inevitable future miseries.

But though the moralizing tradition, centring on the idea
of civic virtue opposed by luxury, was one powerful strain
in social and political analysis in the eighteenth century,

it was not the only one. From the early part of the century onwards, in political and moral debate, it had been challenged by another way of thinking, which tried to establish the legitimacy and to defend the benefits of 'opulence', particularly in association with commerce and industry, the latter of which still carried the moral connotation of 'industriousness'. This defence could take essentially two forms, though they were often blended in complicated ways. One was to assert that the industrious life of merchants and artisans generated its own moral habits, distinct from the patriotic virtue of the citizen-soldier. The other was to accept a measure of disjunction between virtue and public benefits. The life of men in society might simply be too complex for any straightforward correlation between virtue and social well-being. Men created the fabric of civilization and social order not out of benevolence or patriotism, but as the unforeseen consequences of their pursuit of private interests.

'Private vices, public benefits': the Mandevillian paradox

This is the defence of commerce and civilized opulence (a necessary word, to avoid the more pejorative term 'luxury') found in David Hume and in Adam Smith's *The Wealth of Nations* (1776). Gibbon later wrote that he was proud to cite the latter 'as the work of a sage and a friend' (2.483 n.15). But though his references to it are almost invariably approving, he obviously remained slightly uneasy. He paid his tribute to 'the strong ray of philosophic light [which] has broke from Scotland in our own day' (6.445 n.89), but elsewhere we are told that Smith 'proves, perhaps too severely, that the most salutary effects have flowed from the meanest and most selfish causes' (7.298 n.104). The source of Gibbon's uneasiness was an idea with which Smith himself would not have cared to be too closely associated. Gibbon referred to it when he spoke in his *Memoir*, with a disapproval which seems entirely sincere, of 'the licentious doctrine that private vices are public benefits' (M 22). What was at issue here was nothing less than a prizing apart of morals and public happiness, and it could take the form of an aggressive paradox which many found disturbing. The remark from Gibbon's *Memoir* quoted above referred to the work in which the paradox had been most uncompromisingly and satirically exploited, Bernard de Mandeville's *The Fable of the Bees* (1714). It was from Mandeville that the slogan 'private vices, public benefits' derived. The *Fable* tried to show that the rigorous and universal practice of what were taken to be the moral virtues of restraint and self-denial would produce unemployment and general impoverishment, while vanity and luxury and self-interest, on the contrary, promoted the well-being of all, stimulating consumption and providing goods and services.

Gibbon did not accept this paradox in its strict, Mandevillian form. Though he denounced Christian asceticism, there was still much, as we have seen, of the old, classical, republican cult of stern simplicity and hardy patriotism in his account of the corruption of Roman civilization. But as we have also seen (above, p. 46), his essential moderation and subtlety of mind recoiled from the extremes of the 'patriotic' position. Classical political moralizing is strongly present in the *Decline and Fall*. In a good many places it dominates it. But it does not wholly possess it. There is a Smithian or even, one is sometimes inclined to say, a Mandevillian, strain present too, which both gives an additional subtlety and complexity to Gibbon's explanations, and prevents the message of the entire work from being one of pessimism.

Recognition of the ambiguity of human motive, and with

it the possibility that beneficial consequences may flow from morally dubious impulses, is one of the most characteristic features of Gibbon's work. It is, of course, an Augustan theme, as in Pope again, for example:

> What crops of wit and honesty appear
> From spleen, from obstinacy, hate or fear!
> See anger zeal and fortitude supply;
> Even avarice prudence: sloth philosophy . . .
> The same ambition can destroy or save
> And make a patriot as it makes a slave.
>
> (*Essay on Man*, Epistle 2, 185–8, 201–2)

In Gibbon, even when we are first introduced to the key concept of civic virtue, there is an important qualification of virtue by 'interest': 'That public virtue, which among the ancients was denominated patriotism, is derived from a strong sense of our own interest in the preservation and prosperity of the free government of which we are members' (1.10). Here there is a mixture, but hardly a paradox. Elsewhere the contrast of motive and effect, the paradoxes inherent in the 'philosophic' search for underlying causes, and the recognition of the possible importance of unintended consequences, are emphasized: 'In the present imperfect state of society, luxury, though it may proceed from vice or folly, seems to be the only means that can correct the unequal distribution of property' (1.53). Civil society itself, being founded on the institution of property, is grounded in a necessary act of public wrong:

> In the progress from primitive equity to final injustice, the steps are silent, the shades are almost imperceptible, and the absolute monopoly is guarded by positive laws and artificial reason. The active, insatiate principle of

self-love can alone supply the arts of life and the wages of industry. (4.485)

This is an unusually direct statement, occurring in Gibbon's account of Roman law, but the paradoxes are freely scattered. The equal distribution of inheritance is 'that just but pernicious law' (6.494 n.15). Even absolutism may have its benefits: 'The tyrant of Rome was often the benefactor of the provinces', because the absolute ruler finds 'that the interest of society is inseparably connected with his own' (4.452). Freedom, on the other hand, may be not so much the reward of virtue as the consolation of wretchedness: 'The native Caledonians preserved, in the northern extremity of the island, their wild independence, for which they were not less indebted to their poverty than their valour' (1.5).

Paradox, irony, and ambiguity

It is worth observing here how far Gibbon's ironies at the expense of Christianity, which were discussed earlier, represent a kind of extension, an additional ironic twist, to the Mandevillian paradox of 'private vices, public benefits'. Christianity, supposedly an undoubted benefit, owed its successful introduction more to the vices, intolerance, fanaticism and superstition of its evangelists, than to their virtues. Divine truth was propagated by fallible human agents whose motives were almost always mixed and often discreditable: 'the force of truth was on this occasion assisted by the influence of temporal advantages' (2.9). Sometimes, again, the direction of the paradox can be reversed; the disastrous consequence is acknowledged and ironically attributed to the highest motives, as in the case of the monks who 'devoutly tortured the enemy of Christ and Saint Cyril' (5.120). But of course in Gibbon's treatment of Christianity the Mandevillian paradox has been given an additional turn, an extra level of irony: the benefit may not even be beneficial; the propagation of Christianity is seen as a very dubious good.

Ambiguity, in fact—ambiguity of benefits and of motives—is a pervasive and deliberately implanted element in the *Decline and Fall*, and the morally ambiguous character of civilization is only an aspect of it. A recurrent and often noticed feature of Gibbon's writing, for example, is the use of two contrasting terms betweeen which the judgement of the historian is, or appears to be, held in suspense: 'The palace, nay the bedchamber, of the pope was adorned, or polluted, by the visits of his female favourites' (7.86). No single perspective, it is insinuated, is adequate to the historian's task of description and judgement. Standards are various and actions and events many-faceted. Very often the contrasting pair consist of two imputed motives, and the ambiguity may be either in the mind of the agent or the justified hesitation of the historian: 'the credulity or the prudence of Gregory . . .' (5.36). There are numerous such examples in the *Decline and Fall*. 'The avarice or humanity' of Philip Augustus ransoms his prisoners (6.349 n. 77). In a slightly different example, the war was protracted 'by the skill or timidity of the combatants' (2.238). In his *Memoir* Gibbon even applies the doubt to himself. 'I am too modest, or too proud, to rate my own value by that of my associates' (M 178). Language is slippery and we are not omniscient even in relation to ourselves: 'Oft, in the passions' wild rotation tost,/Our spring of action to ourselves is lost' (Pope, *Essay on Man*, Epistle 1. 41–2).

The cumulative effect of such calculated ambiguities on the tone of Gibbon's history is profound, carrying it to levels of sophistication outside the range of neoclassical republican moralizing. The calm, balanced sentences express a view of life which, for all its precision and confidence, is permeated by an awareness of the complexity and ambivalence of human affairs. Men's most important actions proceed from mixed motives and are of doubtful consequence. Virtue and vice are unequally distributed but hardly ever mutually exclusive. Out of evil sometimes comes good, and *vice versa*. Civilization is a precious but precarious achievement, and in some respects a morally equivocal one.

Industry and progress: the grounds of optimism

But it is partly because the relations between virtue and prosperity, luxury and corruption, are less straightforward than neoclassical, republican pessimism would suggest, that there is hope. The heroic patriotism of the citizen-soldier of antiquity may inevitably be lost with the growth of a commercial civilization:

> The progress of manufactures and commerce insensibly collects a large multitude within the walls of a city; but these citizens are no longer soldiers, and the arts which adorn and improve the state of civil society corrupt the habits of military life. (3.74)

But Montesquieu had held, and the Scots had continued the argument, that prosperity need only be fatal when it is linked with conquest and idleness. Industrious habits might be protection against corruption and enervation. Gibbon agreed: 'luxury . . . is always fatal except to an industrious people' (4.352). Useful arts are preserved even through ages of barbarism when learning, letters and political freedom have been lost, and civilized Europe has now forged the weapons which can defend it against any future inroads of barbarism:

> We cannot be displeased that . . . an industrious people

should be protected by these arts which survive and supply the decay of military virtue. Canon and fortifications now form an impregnable barrier against the Tartar horse; and Europe is secure from any future irruption of Barbarians; since before they can conquer, they must cease to be barbarous.

('General Observations', 4.166)

In the *Decline and Fall* Gibbon's account of the revival of civilization in Europe is less clear-cut than his earlier diagnosis of its fall. It is composed of various elements, of which an account of the decay of feudalism and the rise of a new urban life on the basis of commerce and manufactures, is only one, and not the most prominent. Another is a Whig constitutionalism, based on the idea of a balance of powers. The feudal form of society into which the barbarian kingdoms settle, though violent and anarchic, possesses a vigour and spirit of liberty lacking in the uniformity of the Roman administration even at its height. Even the Catholic Church and the Papacy are rather grudgingly allowed some part in the consolidation of a new civilized order in Europe. In none of this is there the reiterated emphasis or crisp elegance of Gibbon's largely neoclassical, republican, and moralizing explanations of the fall of the Roman Empire. In the eighteenth-century debates around the ideas of progress and corruption, Gibbon's allegiance was given, by temperament and conviction, to the former, but it is hard to avoid the conclusion that he was more intellectually at home with the latter. Nevertheless, the presence of optimism and even jubilation is a vital ingredient in giving the tone and outline of the *Decline and Fall*. If Gibbon never fully succeeded in settling the account and working out the relationship between civilization and corruption, the same might be said of many of his contemporaries, including Adam Smith.

8 'A possession in perpetuity'

Narrative in the Decline and Fall

To present a vast historical work like the *Decline and Fall*, as I have done, chiefly in terms of its organizing concepts and the explanations it offers, is necessarily to travesty it: to reveal the bones is to make hard, angular, dry and summary what in the experience of reading is enjoyed as flexible, rich and leisurely. Gibbon's book is an immense piece of historical architecture; appreciation of its intellectual and imaginative design is part of the pleasure of reading it, but so is surrendering to the purposeful but unforced flow of a dense and varied narrative.

Narrative is by nature hard to illustrate and impossible adequately to abbreviate; it can only be experienced at length. The reader who wants simply to sample Gibbon as narrator might begin with one of the most tautly written, closely textured of his accounts, Chapter 22, which deals with the rising of the troops of the future Emperor Julian the Apostate in Gaul, their march to the east with Julian at their head to challenge the Emperor Constantine and, after the latter's death by natural causes, the proclamation and triumph of Julian as Emperor. So summarized, there is, in the context of the *Decline and Fall*, nothing remarkable about these events; such occurrences were commonplace. But Gibbon here had an unusually detailed and reliable source, the historian Ammianus Marcellinus, who was an intimate of the Emperor Julian, as well as—rare in an emperor—Julian's own writings. Gibbon took full advantage of them. But even though Ammianus was one of the best of the ancient historians used by Gibbon, and the latter paid tribute to his impartiality, there still remained much for Gibbon to do in the shaping and dramatic organization of his chapter. He described his task, elsewhere, referring to less promising materials, as 'to extract a rational narrative from the dark, concise and various hints' of his sources; 'A gentle pressure and paraphrase of their words is no violence' (4.197 n.99). Even in the case of Ammianus he complained of his 'coarse and undistinguishing pencil' (3.19) and of 'the disorder and perplexity of his narrative' (3.119 n.93). To compare Gibbon and Ammianus on the same events in Gibbon's twenty-second chapter is to appreciate how artfully and imaginatively Gibbon organized and presented the stages of his drama. the Emperor's suspicions of his successful and virtuous young general; the despair of Julian's Gaulish auxiliaries and their families on receiving the imperial order to leave their homes and serve in Persia; Julian's own dismay at the defencelessness of Gaul; and the 'respectful violence' of the soldiers as they force Julian to assume the imperial title. At the head of a small body of picked troops he 'plunged into the recesses of the Marcian or black forest, which conceals the sources of the Danube; and, for many days, the fate of Julian was unknown to the world' (2.410). His re-emergence to secure the passage of the Danube, his triumphal march into Thrace, and his letters of justification to the Athenians, mark the transition from the soldier guarding the frontier of the Rhine to the philosopher-emperor, with his vain nostalgia for the religion and philosophy of Greece. Gibbon's depiction of Julian's character, with its virtues and inconsistencies, its austerity mingled with vanity and ostentation, is the most famous of his portraits, and his epitaph for the Emperor whose nostalgia he shared is moving in its superbly calculated, ironic understatement:

> The remains of Julian were interred at Tarsus, in Cilicia;
> But his stately tomb which arose in that city, on the
> banks of the cold and limpid Cyndus, was displeasing to
> his faithful friends, who loved and revered the memory
> of that extraordinary man. The philosopher expressed a
> very reasonable wish that the disciple of Plato might
> have reposed amid the graves of the academy: while the
> soldiers exclaimed in bolder accents that the ashes of
> Julian should have been mingled with those of Caesar in
> the field of Mars, and among the ancient monuments of
> Roman virtue. The history of princes does not very
> frequently renew the example of a similar competition.
> (2.529–30)

The chapter we have considered in outline is a
particularly good example of taut, dramatic construction
and of artfully selected episode and detail. For an equally
remarkable example, of quite another kind, representing
the scope and scale of Gibbon's work and the extraordinary
control he was able to keep of his diverse materials, we
might take Chapter 40. Here we have almost a panorama
of the known world in the sixth century, and its historic
transitions, seen from the perspective of Constantinople.

In this one, extraordinary, chapter, we have the early
careers of the Emperor Justinian and his scandalous
Empress Theodora, the riots of the blue and green
factions—'the license, without the freedom, of demo-
cracy'—of the Hippodrome in Constantinople, the development of the silk trade with China, the building of the
great church of St Sophia, and the final suppression of the
pathetic remnants of two great forces which had shaped the
ancient world, the schools of Athens, where Plato and
Aristotle had taught almost a thousand years before, and

the consulship of Rome. There is nothing perfunctory here; the detail at times is dense. Yet there is no sense of a jumble or inventory either; the transitions of subject to subject are smooth, natural, apparently effortless. What the chapter conveys is not strain but sheer enjoyment. Gibbon was equally responsive to the pathos of the past and to the appeal of the exotic. His language, when discussion of trade routes takes him to the Far East, has a Miltonic splendour: 'Ceylon, Serendib, or Taprobana, was divided between two hostile princes; one of whom possessed the mountains, the elephants, and the luminous carbuncle; and the other enjoyed the more solid riches of domestic industry, foreign trade, and the capacious harbour of Trinquemale, which received and dismissed the fleets of the East and the West' (4.232).

Gibbon's prose: diction and syntax

Gibbon's prose is, of course, measured, studied and proudly self-conscious; it aims not at unobtrusiveness but at effect, in choice of diction and control of rhythm. But the effects are subtly, sometimes startlingly, varied. He can, as we have seen, be ample and grand, sometimes even in dealing with abstractions. He had no sympathy with Platonic philosophy, for example, but no neo-Platonist could surpass the words he finds for the sublime concept of a First Cause of the universe and the mystery of how 'a Being purely incorporeal could execute that perfect model and mould with a plastic hand the rude and independent chaos' (2.335). The slightly ironic precision of 'rude and independent' acquires a subtle suggestiveness in the *Decline and Fall*, being the same adjectives frequently applied to the barbarians.

Abstraction is, of course, one of the most characteristic features of Gibbon's writing; abstract nouns replace

97

adjectives and adverbs, in Augustan fashion, to achieve an elegant compression: 'the prudence', 'the clemency', 'the compassion'. These can be used either as antitheses, expressing the historian's qualifications or hesitation (see above, p. 91) or cumulatively: 'The heart of Theodosius was softened by the tears of beauty; his affections were insensibly engaged by the graces of youth and innocence; the art of Justina managed and directed the impulse of passion; and the celebration of the royal nuptials was the assurance and signal of the civil war' (3.164–5). This is something like a standard narrative pattern. As we have seen, if balance is one typical feature of Gibbon's manner, the management of climax, as here, is another. A succession of short related statements, separated by semi-colons, is rounded off crisply, grandly, elegiacally, or ironically, as the sense requires. Being climactic, such sentences can easily, of course, be made deliberately anticlimactic or bathetic. Gibbon's description of the conquest of Britain is an amusing variation on this pattern, a sequence of bathetic superlatives followed surprisingly by a genuine climax: 'After a war of about forty years, undertaken by the most stupid, maintained by the most dissolute, and terminated by the most timid of all the emperors, the far greater part of the island submitted to the Roman yoke' (1.3–4).

But if Gibbon's manner is often abstract, ample, and cumulative, it can also be particular and sharply visualized. Unfortunately his extended descriptions, of the Colosseum, the palace of Diocletian (derived from the architect Robert Adam), the site of Byzantium, the buildings of Rome as seen by the Gothic king Theodoric, are too long to be quoted. He was susceptible, as one would expect of the author of the *Decline and Fall*, which had been conceived among the ruins of the Capitol, to poignant contrasts of grandeur and desolation: 'The Ionic temple of Aesculapius is encompassed with Moorish huts; and the cattle now graze in the midst of an amphitheatre, under the shade of Corinthian columns' (4.298). Sometimes the touch of the particular is effective in its unexpectedness: every night in the monasteries of Egypt 'a rustic horn or trumpet, the signal of devotion, twice interrupted the vast silence of the desert' (4.71). Gibbon's metaphorical effects too can have an arresting boldness: 'every wind scattered round the empire the leaves of controversy; and the voice of the combatants in a sonorous theatre re-echoed in the cells of Palestine and Egypt' (5.113).

Gibbon can be vivid and he can also be terse. Sometimes he is deliberately sententious, as in 'the last temptation of virtuous minds, an indiscreet and intemperate zeal for justice' (2.285). Often, however, we simply get an epigrammatic characterization: 'Justinian was so profuse that he could not be liberal' (4.236) or 'their friendship was venal, their faith inconstant, their enmity capricious' (5.320). Such brevity lends itself, above all, to dismissiveness, and it is employed by Gibbon with deadly effect in his footnotes. It is hard to imagine a more unanswerable casualness than the dismissal of the Greek historians who 'displayed the love, rather than the talent, of fiction' (3.387 n.74) or the verdict on St Augustine: 'his learning was too often borrowed, and his arguments are too often his own' (3.211 n.86). More purely mischievous is the annotation on the death of the pagan emperor Galerius: the Christian historians Lactantius and Eusebius 'describe the symptoms and progress of his disorder with singular accuracy and apparent pleasure' (1.411 n.43).

Gibbon's footnotes: the fraternity of scholarship

Gibbon's footnotes, in fact, are one of the acknowledged

delights of the *Decline and Fall*. They provide much more than a guide to Gibbon's sources; they are a commentary on the text. The latter is formal, polished and grand— though ironic mischief lurks there too. But the notes are often garrulous, unbuttoned, highly personal and, of course, funny. In the text we have the calm, judicial assurance of the historian; in the notes the scholar's chortles, camaraderie, testiness, and smut, as he addresses the reader and offers fraternal congratulations and rebukes to his colleagues, ancient and modern. It would be possible to compile a comprehensive and entertaining critical bibliography of European historical writing from the second century AD to the eighteenth century from Gibbon's notes alone. As the chapter titles record the march of events as the great work rolls onwards, so the notes (and occasionally the text) register the successive arrival of fresh batches of authorities, each greeted with discriminating—and often damning—adjectives, the more reputable being given, in due course, an appreciative farewell salute. Gibbon's notes have not only the confidence of familiarity—'his usual minuteness', 'his habitual accuracy', 'a strange departure from his usual character'—but also its warmth and its contempt: 'a judicious and candid historian', 'his prolix and florid history', 'that contemptible author'. Gibbon was proud of the extent of his knowledge of the writings of the Church Fathers, and not above showing off: 'Ambrose could act better than he could write. His compilations are destitute of taste or genuis; without the spirit of Tertullian, the copious elegance of Lactantius, the lively wit of Jerom, or the grave energy of Augustin' (3.175 n.98). Sometimes the note is weary: 'I will neither hear nor reconcile the long and contradictory accounts of the Abbé Dubos and the Comte de Buat about the wars of Burgundy' (4.187 n.59). One of the—frequently critical—references to Montesquieu gives the merest flick of condescension: 'The president Montesquieu had formed the plan of an history of Theodoric, which at a distance might appear a rich and interesting subject' (4.180 n.32).

But though Gibbon sometimes complains of tedium or weariness, the most lasting impression one carries away from his footnotes, apart from scrupulous critical intelligence and an inimitable wit, is of the amazing comprehensiveness and detail of his learning, and his insatiable factual curiosity. So far as he is able, the notes to the chapters on Persia, Abyssinia or the Arabs are as conscientiously and critically minute in matters of geography or chronology as those on Italy. Gibbon always tries to be exact about dimensions or numbers. 'On the most correct plans of Constantinople, I know not how to measure more than 4,000 paces. Yet Villehardouin computes the space at three leagues. If his eye were not deceived, he must reckon by the old Gallic league of 1500 paces, which might still be used in Champagne' (6.396 n.79).

Organization: the historian as impresario

Such minuteness, combined with the immense perspectives of the *Decline and Fall*, all seen through an urbane, controlling, personal vision, is awesome to contemplate; that additionally it is all embodied in a prose whose poise, alertness and precision scarcely falter, as the majestic sentences and paragraphs roll on, century after century, and the fastidiously chosen words mount in their hundreds of thousands, is almost miraculous. Gibbon was intensely aware of his own feats of control over vast masses of material and great tracts of space and time, and proudly drew attention to them. He deliberately sacrificed chronology to thematic coherence when required, in a fashion whose originality it is hard now for us to appreciate: 'We shall consult order and perspicuity by pursuing not so much the doubtful arrangement of dates as the more natural distribution of subjects' (1.254).

The conflation of narrative and event, historian, and historical agent, was a conceit which always attracted Gibbon, but his earlier uses of it in the *Decline and Fall* are playful and ironic: 'Before we enter on the memorable reign of that prince, it will be proper to punish and dismiss the unworthy brother of Numerian' (1.349), or 'M. de Voltaire . . . unsupported by either fact or probability, has generously bestowed the Canary islands on the Roman empire' (1.26 n.95). But as the work advances and the scale widens, Gibbon becomes, more overtly and solemnly, not just the teller but the organizer and conductor of the immense events he describes: 'the following nations will pass before our eyes'; 'I shall lead . . .', 'I shall return . . .', 'I now descend . . .'. And finally, with his work nearing its end, 'The remaining fragments of the Greek kingdom in Europe and Asia I shall abandon to the Turkish armies' (7.203). 'The historian of the Roman empire', in laying down his office, gives his concluding pages, only half ironically, the air of a deathbed: 'For myself, it is my wish to depart in charity with all mankind; nor am I willing, in these last moments, to offend even the pope and clergy of Rome' (7.299).

Gibbon and the Decline and Fall: *time, death, and consciousness*

It was as though the author and his work had become one, and in a sense this was true: the *Decline and Fall* was the fullest and truest portrayal he could give of his own mind. He was intensely aware of the imaginative act of reading, above all of history, as the extension of our lives. The man of learning 'by reading and reflection, multiplies his own experience, and lives in a distant age and remote countries' (1.218). He set the same thought at the opening of his autobiography: 'Our imagination is always active to enlarge the narrow circle in which nature has confined us' (M 3). The contrast of the death of the individual, and the narrowness of his life, with the boundless life of the mind, and the enduring influence which is recognized by fame, is in a sense the most fundamental polarity of all those to be found in the *Decline and Fall*; that is, it is what, at the most abstract level, Gibbon's history is 'about', and in that sense his writing of it is another act that the history invites us to contemplate. The identification is very plain in its final chapter, which, like its conception, is a meditation on the ruins of Rome. Aware of the monumental immensity of the book he has just read, the alert reader can hardly miss the suggestion that Gibbon is talking about his own life's work, and assimilating it, here not so much with pride as with pathos, to the Roman Empire. The reference to 'man' becomes individual rather than collective:

> The art of man is able to construct monuments far more permanent than the narrow span of his own existence; yet these monuments, like himself, are perishable and frail; and in the boundless annals of time his life and labours must equally be measured as a fleeting moment. (7.305)

Gibbon's thoughts on laying down his pen, at Lausanne in 1787, or those he thought it appropriate to record, were, not surprisingly, of fame and of death:

> I have presumed to mark the moment of conception; I shall now commemorate the hour of my final deliverance. It was on the day, or rather night, of the

27th of June, 1787, between the hours of eleven and twelve, that I wrote the last lines of the last page, in a summer-house in my garden. After laying down my pen, I took several turns in a *berceau*, or covered walk of acacias, which commands a prospect of the country, the lake and the mountains. The air was temperate, the sky was serene, the silver orb of the moon was reflected from the waters, and all nature was silent. I will not dissemble the first emotion of joy on the recovery of my freedom, and, perhaps, the establishment of my fame. But my pride was soon humbled, and a sober melancholy was spread over my mind, by the idea that I had taken an everlasting leave of an old and agreeable companion, and that whatever might be the future fate of my *History*, the life of the historian must be short and precarious. (M 180)

Fame

It seems that Gibbon had only the faintest possible belief, if any at all, in the possibility of a life after death: 'The present is a fleeting moment, the past is no more; and our prospect of futurity is dark and doubtful' (M 188). We sense approval when he writes of the pagan philosophers' acceptance 'as an obvious, though melancholy position, that the fatal stroke of our dissolution releases us from the calamities of life; and that those can no longer suffer who no longer exist' (1.19). The only kind of immortality which made any sense was fame, and Gibbon wrote in a tradition, that of the ancient narrative historians, in which the concept of fame was a weighty and vivid one.

But Gibbon was no hero-worshipper of men of action. Writing from sources which often indulged in extremes of flattery or vilification, he saw his task as being to moderate these judgements and bring them closer to probable truth;

it was a maxim of his, derived from Bayle, that the historian could trust in the virtues acknowledged by a man's enemies and the vices admitted by his admirers. It is not really true—it is certainly an exaggeration—that, as used to be said when detraction of the eighteenth century was fashionable, Gibbon judged the men of past ages exclusively by the standards of his own time; he made a serious effort to understand the mentality of religious enthusiasm displayed in an historical event like the First Crusade, and to balance the probable elements of belief and self-interest in the conversion of Constantine. But he was certainly no admirer of mere success. In that sense, his judgements are extra-historical. The emperor who attracts his warmest sympathy, Julian the Apostate, was a philosopher as well as a man of action, whose reign was dedicated to a futile attempt to turn the tide of history and revive a dying paganism. Even Julian is criticized for taking too solemnly the role of the philosopher, in the ancient sense, as a man scornfully above the petty decorum of everyday life. Gibbon often prefers men when they step outside their historic roles and reveal ordinary humane feeling; this is particularly true, of course, of saints: 'The title of saint has been added to his name; but the tenderness of his heart and the elegance of his genius reflect a more pleasing lustre on the memory of Gregory Nazianzen' (2.151); and, more ironically, St Bernard 'seems to have preserved as much reason and humanity as may be reconciled with the character of a saint' (6.333). But Gibbon was himself scornful of the littleness of mere worldly ambition, in a way that he thought of as philosophic, but which occasionally can hardly escape an almost religious loftiness: 'the grave is ever beside the throne; the success of a criminal is almost instantly followed by the loss of his prize' (5.243). More often he conveys the same judgement with his own inimitable dismissiveness: 'Such troops were a feeble defence against the approach of Aurelian; and it seems almost unnecessary to relate that Firmus was routed, taken, tortured, and put to death' (1.310).

The opposite of such scornful dismissals, the respectful recognition of true fame, is reserved more for men of thought than men of action: Tacitus, for example, 'the philosophic historian whose writings will instruct the last generations of mankind' (1.319–20). The treasury of civilization outlasts individuals and even empires. Fielding's novel, 'the Romance of Tom Jones, that exquisite picture of human manners will outlive the palace of the Escurial and the Imperial Eagle of the house of Austria' (M 5). It is the legitimate pride of the author to think 'that one day his mind will be familiar to the grandchildren of those who are yet unborn' (M 188), and in it Gibbon vested his only hopes of immortality: 'In old age, the consolation of hope is reserved for the tenderness of parents, who commence a new life in their children; the faith of enthusiasts, who sing Hallelujahs above the clouds; and the vanity of authors, who presume the immortality of their name and writings' (M 189).

These concluding words of Gibbon's autobiography contain perhaps, as is appropriate in Gibbon's case, more than one layer of irony. It is ironic at the expense of the crudity of religious hopes and of the possible fatuity of those of the individual author for his fame, but the preacher's word 'vanity' may also hint at the transience even of fame and of all human works. *Ars longa vita brevis*, life is short, art is enduring, but even endurance is not immortality. Seen in the light of this, as well as of the shortness of individual human lives, including the historian's, the latter's proud, conscious exposition and control of the great perspectives of history becomes something like an act of defiance, an imposition of meaning on the flux of time.

History, 'philosophy', and epic

It is in this sense that the historian is a 'philosophic observer': he looks down with 'a smile of pity and contempt on the crimes and follies of human ambition, so eager, in a narrow span, to grasp at a precarious and short-lived enjoyment' (5.242). Gibbon used the word 'philosophic' in a number of related senses. Some of them are particularly characteristic of his time, as when it is used as the opposite of bigotry and fanaticism, or to indicate the search for the underlying causes of events. But there are also more traditional, classical senses, one of which is a stoic acceptance of the inevitable and the recognition of one's ignorance; it is for this reason that the philosophic spirit is at the opposite pole from superstition, which is facile belief in what cannot be known, born of the excesses of fear and hope. But the philosophic stance, a realism which is necessarily in some degree melancholy, also contains possibilities of a proper pride and exaltation, in its transcendence of the petty circumstances of life and of individual desires and ambitions. In this sense, for Gibbon, 'philosophic historian' is almost a repetition of terms:

> It is thus that the experience of history exalts and enlarges the horizon of our intellectual view. In a composition of some days, a perusal of some hours, six hundred years have rolled away, and the duration of a life or reign is contracted to a fleeting moment . . . and our immortal reason survives and disclaims the sixty phantoms of beings who have passed before our eyes, and faintly dwell on our remembrance. (5.242)

Author and reader are united, within a short space of time—days or hours—in a fellowship of reason and imagination which rises above time not by denying it but by contemplating it. The triumph of time epitomized in the ruins of Rome, and the triumph over time embodied in the history conceived among them, were Gibbon's profoundest concerns, as was his stoic awareness of the paradox that the latter was only temporary.

It is this awareness which gives heroic significance to the historian's rational control over the vast temporal and cultural perspectives of the *Decline and Fall*, and this in turn is what gives Gibbon's history its epic quality. E. M. W. Tillyard, in his book *The English Epic and its Background* (London, 1954), devoted the last part of it to the *Decline and Fall*, putting Gibbon in the company of Virgil and Milton. Tillyard distinguished, as the central characteristics of an epic, its high seriousness, its amplitude and inclusiveness, the control of the author's will over his material, and the epic's expression, not just of the author's feelings and beliefs, but of those of a whole period or culture. Few would quarrel with the inclusion of Gibbon on any of these counts, or with the notion that *The Decline and Fall of the Roman Empire* is the epic of the European Enlightenment and of Augustan England as Milton's poem is that of the European Renaissance, Dante's of the high Middle Ages and Virgil's of Augustan Rome.

Reading Gibbon: *The* Decline and Fall *in historical perspective*

But the last point, the way Gibbon's history, in its own unique fashion and as much as any single work can, epitomizes the thought and feelings of its age, raises, for the modern reader, the question of its abiding value as history. It is absurd to speak of reading Gibbon simply 'as literature', or worse still 'for his style', if by this is meant a kind of tasting of choice passages. Gibbon's book is literature, but it is also history, and it is as history—whatever that means—that it has to be read. J. B. Bury's edition of 1912, cited here throughout, gives the corrections on matters of fact, so far as the scholarship of the early twentieth century could supply them. On the whole Gibbon's accuracy is no less astonishing than his other qualities. Of course, the countless specialist scholars who now divide the matter of the *Decline and Fall*, often with extreme minuteness, among them, are collectively more knowledgeable, but there is no question of Gibbon's work ever being superseded by a comparable survey. Gibbon's particular biases are easy enough to recognize and allow for: his identification with the senatorial class of Rome and his distaste for the reorganizations of Diocletian and Constantine; his military conservatism, with its nostalgia for the legions of the Republic and early Empire and its suspicion of newfangled heavy cavalry and artillery; his general prejudice against Byzantium—his weakest spot; and his hatred of monks.

The perspectives and interests of modern historians are sometimes different, of course, but this provides a reason for reading Gibbon, not for neglecting him. Reading a great historical writer of the past furthers the end that all historical writing or reading may be said to have in view: the overcoming of the cultural parochialism of our own times. To read such a work is never, whether we are aware of it or not, a simple cultural experience. There is a complex interaction between Gibbon's material, his own mind and all that went to shape it, the eighteenth-century world he addressed and in some measure reflected, and ourselves as readers. Reading the *Decline and Fall* is so rewarding precisely because of this many-layered texture, the encounter it offers with other worlds, including the one that was most immediately his own, the eighteenth century.

But just as Gibbon, like any other historian, even the most boring, is not simply a transparent medium for the facts, neither is he just an 'eighteenth-century' screen framing them and imposing its patterns on them, but one tinted with many influences, only some of them distinctively contemporary, set in a unique configuration. The eighteenth century, like any other period of high culture, offered an intellectual treasury of past and present influences to be explored and exploited, and Gibbon was responsive to far more of them than most authors. Many epochs of European cultural experience went into the making of the *Decline and Fall*. Through Cicero and Tacitus above all, Gibbon, like many of his contemporaries, was imbued with the aristocratic, republican attitudes and literary models of the Roman senatorial class of the late Republic and early Empire. Far more than most of his contemporaries, he was the heir of the scholarship of the Renaissance and the learning of the Reformation and Counter-Reformation, as well as the beneficiary of the antiquarian scholarship and travel literature of his own and the immediately preceding generations. He inherited the love of polish and balance, and the zest for good sense and proportion, of the English Augustan writers of the early eighteenth century. He acquired something of the anticlerical, polemical edge of the French *philosophes*, even though he sometimes disapproved of it. His understanding of history was crucially influenced by Montesquieu's search for underlying causes, and the contemporary, distinctively Scottish and Smithian doctrine of 'unintended consequences'. But none of this is allowed an undue preponderance. Gibbon is never for long merely dignified or merely learned, just urbane or polemical or explanatory. His work is not derivative; it is a highly personal summation, expressed in an unmistakable voice.

Many of the complaints made against Gibbon's history since it was published, of his irreligion and his supposed indecency, now seem beside the point. Christians today are more tolerant, more hardened, or more sceptical than their Georgian or Victorian predecessors. As for indecency, few readers now are likely, as Gibbon might put it, in an age of less learning and more extensive license, to find their delicacy wounded, or their prurience excited, by footnotes in the obscurity of a learned language, though some of Gibbon's innuendoes remain funny. But even in what is usually the trough of an author's reputation, in the generation or two after his death, when the Evangelical and Romantic movements were at their height, Gibbon remained famous and formidable. The Reverend Dr Bowdler paid him the oblique compliment of choosing the *Decline and Fall*, after the works of Shakespeare, on which to practise the craft to which he gave his name. The two leading Romantic poets of the second generation, Shelley and Byron, paid a visit in 1816 to Gibbon's house in Lausanne. The summer-house was already derelict; the house itself is now gone. Shelley afterwards wrote disapprovingly of Gibbon's 'cold and unimpassioned spirit', but Byron plucked some acacia leaves from the terrace where Gibbon walked, and in *Childe Harold* hailed him as 'the lord of irony', placing him with Rousseau and Voltaire as the spirits of the lake of Geneva, gigantic minds

who sought and found, by dangerous roads,
A path to perpetuity of fame.
                    (*Childe Harold's Pilgrimage*, III cv)

Sources and further reading

A list of Gibbon's chief works is given in the Abbreviations at the front of this book. A complete list of all his writings can be found in J. E. Norton, *A Bibliography of the Works of Edward Gibbon* (Oxford, 1970), which also gives an account of their contemporary reception. Only a proportion of the works used in the preparation of this book can be acknowledged here. The following are those which will be found particularly useful:

On Gibbon himself: two biographical studies, D. M. Low, *Edward Gibbon, 1737–1794* (London, 1937) and Patricia B. Craddock, *Young Edward Gibbon, Gentleman of Letters* (Baltimore, 1982). Of general studies of Gibbon, the most balanced and generally useful is David P. Jordan, *Edward Gibbon and his Roman Empire* (Illinois, 1971). G. M. Young, *Gibbon* (London, 1932), is readable and perceptive. There are some distinguished and useful essays in G. W. Bowerstock, John Clive, and Stephen R. Graubard (eds.) *Edward Gibbon and the Fall of the Roman Empire* (Cambridge, Mass. and London, 1977).

For further reading on the themes discussed in particular chapters of this book, the following are the most authoritative and helpful:

Chapter 3. For Gibbon's place in European historical scholarship in his own time, two classic articles by Arnaldo Momigliano, 'Ancient History and the Antiquarian' and 'Gibbon's Contribution to Historical Method', in *Studies in Historiography* (London, 1966).

Chapter 4. (i) The indispensable source for the concept of republican civic virtue is J. G. A. Pocock, *The*

Machiavellian Moment (Princeton, NJ, 1975). Pocock has applied these ideas to Gibbon in his contribution to the volume by Bowerstock, Clive, and Graubard cited above. See also James William Johnson, *The Formation of English Neo-Classical Thought* (Princeton, NJ, 1967).

(ii) For the concept of 'stages', R. L. Meek, *Social Science and the Ignoble Savage* (Cambridge, 1976) and Pocock 'Gibbon and the Shepherds: The Stages of Society in the *Decline and Fall*', *History of European Ideas*, vol. 2, no. 3, pp. 193–202 (1981).

(iii) Pocock's work is relevant here too. I have also found help in considering the idea of 'civilization' in Sheldon Rothblatt, *Tradition and Change in English Liberal Education* (London, 1976).

On the relations of the ideas of luxury, commerce, and industry in the Scottish Enlightenment, Donald Winch's *Adam Smith's Politics* (Cambridge, 1978) is valuable.

Chapter 5. On questions of style and narrative organization in Gibbon, see Harold L. Bond, *The Literary Art of Edward Gibbon* (Oxford, 1960), and Leo Braudy, *Narrative Form in History and Fiction* (Princeton, NJ, 1970).

Index

OXFORD

PAST MASTERS

A complete list of Oxford Paperbacks, including The World's Classics, Twentieth-Century Classics, OPUS, Oxford Authors, Oxford Shakespeare, and Oxford Paperback Reference, as well as Past Masters, is available from the General Publicity Department, Oxford University Press, Walton Street, Oxford OX2 6DP.

In the USA, complete lists are available from the Paperbacks Marketing Manager, Oxford University Press, 200 Madison Avenue, New York, NY 10016.

MACHIAVELLI Quentin Skinner

Niccolò Machiavelli taught that political leaders must be prepared to do evil that good may come of it, and his name has been a byword ever since for duplicity and immorality. Is his sinister reputation really deserved? In answering this question Quentin Skinner focuses on three major works, *The Prince*, the *Discourses*, and *The History of Florence*, and distils from them an introduction to Machiavelli's doctrines of exemplary clarity.

'without doubt the best short account of the author of "The Prince" that we are likely to see for some time . . . a model of clarity and good judgement' *Sunday Times*

'compulsive reading' *New Society*